THE EDGE

{ Business Performance through Information Technology Leadership }

MANOJ GARG

MICHAEL SCHEUERMAN

The Edge -
Business Performance through Information Technology Leadership

Published by:
Virtual Information Executives, LLC
12639 NW Waker Drive, Portland, OR 97229
www.viellc.com/resources/the-edge
information@viellc.com

ISBN13: 978-0-578-17120-3
Library of Congress Control Number: 2015916688
Also published simultaneously in eBook format
For bulk ordering copies of this book, please contact VIE at information@viellc.
com

Cover design by: BookBaby
Book design by: BookBaby
Printed in the United States of America

Contents

Acknowledgements

We wish to thank all those whose expertise, generously given, has made this book possible: first and foremost, Afton Nelson; without her help and dedication, this book would not have been possible. We would also like to thank our clients who, over the years, have placed their faith in us and allowed us to look deeply into their organizations and learn what we hope is conveyed in this book. We also would like to thank all those who read and commented on the rough drafts of the book. Their input is greatly appreciated and contributed to making this book much better. Lastly, we would like to thank our spouses, who supported us whole-heartedly throughout not only the writing of this book but also through all the years while we garnered the experience needed to write it.

Manoj Garg
Mike Scheuerman
October, 2015

Introduction

Most business executives know that technology is a key ingredient for business success. At the same time, they are baffled by the complexity, costs and challenges in implementing technology methods they are not skilled in.

In most mid-size businesses, executives think of technology as a necessary evil and a cost to be minimized. However, with the right application, technology can increase speed of business dramatically while lowering costs. When leveraged appropriately, technology plays a strategic role in a company, driving business innovation, increasing customer satisfaction, and finding new markets and new revenue sources to drive the top line.

U.S. census from 2014 data reveals that there are around 180,000 firms in the nation with revenues between $10 million and $1 billion annually. These firms typically rely on enterprise-wide software applications, and often deploy specialized technology to stay competitive in their markets. Their C-level executives and key managers keenly understand that technology is strategic, not tactical. They know it's a tool for business success, and continually evolving. But technology is also an occasional mystery to many executives.

They wonder:

- How can IT bring competitive advantage to our company?
- How can IT help drive improved performance of the critical departments in our organization?
- How can IT increase productivity and reduce our need to

hire more people?

- How can IT protect our intellectual property and business secrets?

- Which of all the cool new technologies can help our organization?

- How can we navigate through all these super-expensive IT products and services?

- Is IT helping ensure our compliance with laws and policies?

- Are we capable of selecting—much less implementing—a key software package that's vital to our future business success?

Not understanding or properly implementing Information Technology can cost companies dearly. A McKinsey & Co. study done in 2012 of 5400 large scale IT projects found that 17% of those projects go so badly that they threaten the company's very existence. On average, large IT projects ran 45% over budget and over time, while delivering 56% less value than predicted.

Here's another example: Cover Oregon, a project undertaken by the State of Oregon to implement a Healthcare Exchange, cost taxpayers over $300 million and had to be abandoned due to complexity and project management challenges.

The Edge is a business novel that educates senior business leaders how to get an edge in running their companies through the strategic use of Information Technology. It gives executives the knowledge and tools to guide their company as it transitions from a mid-level to a high-level competitor in the marketplace. It takes the wondering out of the picture and shows business leaders what software applications and specialized technologies can do. Through its narrative, it simultaneously tells the tale of a company and the struggles of the family that runs it, while describing principles of technology management.

For the reader who does not have the time to read the novel, they can skip to the Concepts Tutorial for a quick 30-minute education on how to manage IT for maximum business value.

1

Forging Ahead

Jack flipped on the light in his office and paused for a moment to look around. The picture of his wife and kids still stood watch over the mess of papers on his desk, his leather chair still had that little rip in the seat from the time he forgot about the pen in his back pocket, the wide window still looked out onto the parking lot full of his employees' cars, and the walls were still covered with advertising posters from the last twenty years of Mama Meg's Cookies. The face on every poster, the person the public associated with home-baked goodness, was his mother, Meg McCallister.

It was exactly the same as he'd left it last Friday, but today, just three days later, everything seemed so different now that Meg was gone. Her funeral over the weekend had made final what Jack, until recently, could never have imagined happening. His larger-than-life mother, who seemed like she could go on forever, had turned out to be merely human, just like everyone else.

It had been three years since she'd pulled away from daily operations at Mama Meg's, yet her presence was still felt at every level of the company she built, from Jack's CEO office, all the way down to the drivers who delivered cookies to stores all over the west. How could it not?

As a single mom, Meg had taken her company from her kitchen to a fifteen-thousand-square-foot plant bringing in fifty million dollars a year. Her scrappy determination, along with her sweet-as-pie public persona, made her a well-loved public figure everyone wanted to root for. Jack had learned long ago that even though Margaret McCallister came home to him and his siblings every night, everyone who loved Mama Meg's cookies claimed her as their mother, too.

It had been five years since Jack took the helm as CEO after years of working at the company, but today he felt a touch of the same anxiety he'd had on his first day, unsure of where or what to anchor himself to without his mother's moorings. He turned his attention to the unread email in his inbox. There was one from Marcia Ashcraft, his Vice President of Marketing, about the PR plan for Meg's passing. He flagged it to remind himself to look at it later and clicked open the email from Walt Torbet, his CFO. The attached file had the latest earnings report he hoped would be enough to impress the Board of Directors at the meeting this afternoon.

He scrolled through quickly to the bottom line and his gut clenched: nowhere close to where they needed to be for this time of year. At this rate, they wouldn't meet their quarterly goals, and if the trend continued, their yearly goals were in jeopardy also. The Board was going to eat him alive.

The sales column showed the numbers were up, yet the profits didn't reflect the increased sales. How could that be? The last few months everyone had been working harder than ever. Manufacturing was putting in lots of overtime and purchasing of ingredients was at an all-time high. They were making more cookies than ever. Why didn't it show in the bottom line? Jack didn't know if prices for raw materials were rising, or if they were getting dinged for rush orders from suppliers.

There was a quick knock at Jack's door and his sister Laura, Mama Meg's COO, popped her head in. "Got a minute?" she asked. Her tall frame filled the doorway, but it was her square jaw and wavy, chestnut hair that had always made strangers ask if she and Jack were twins. Years ago, Jack had thought their two-year difference in age had been obvious, but now it wasn't the difference in years that mattered to Jack as much as loyalty and business experience. Laura had plenty of both. Her grey tailored suit belied her easy-going personality the same way Jack's khakis and untucked polo shirt masked his serious nature and tendency to worry.

"Sure. Just reading Walt's report. I don't know how I'm going to sugarcoat this for the Board this afternoon."

Laura stepped in and took a seat across from Jack. "That bad?"

"I'll figure something out." Jack shook his head, uncertain, but determined. Lately it had felt like work was a series of increasingly dramatic crises and he wondered when things would get back to a more routine flow.

"Well, this won't solve your problem with the Board, but I wanted to give you a heads-up before the executive meeting this morning," Laura said, leaning back in her chair. "I just found out we're short some ingredients for the Grocery King order. The forecasting report was off, again. Now I'm stuck buying on the spot market. Emergency ordering is killing our profit margins."

"Can Leslie get you a better sales forecast?" Jack figured he knew the answer to the question. His Vice President of Sales was good at what she did, mostly because she always exceeded expectations. Her relationship with her clients was what kept many of the big customers loyal to Mama Meg's. However, it was her own co-workers who got the short end of the stick, often stuck trying to meet impossible deadlines and scrambling for more ingredients to fill her orders.

"She does her best to estimate, but it's always just that: an estimate." Laura swiped her brown curls behind her ear, shook her head and shrugged. "That means our purchasing decisions are essentially guesses, too. But what are we going to do? That's how we've always done it. We've always managed to get by." She was more resigned than frustrated. "We just need to find a way to adjust to the increased sales. That's a good problem to have, right?"

There had definitely been a few bumps in the road as Mama Meg's responded to their recent growth. It seemed like everything had been going fine. Until it wasn't.

"Now, everything is on hold," Laura continued. "We've got a whole shift sitting around with nothing to do while we break down the line and set it up for another order. Meanwhile, Leslie has to give Grocery King some idea of the ship date, but I have no idea what to tell her."

"I'm sure she can give the client a ballpark ship date. That's always worked in the past."

"I tried that, but these bigger clients don't work that way. Grocery King wants confirmed ship dates so they know exactly when product will be in all their stores."

"Humph." Jack folded his arms across his chest and gazed off into the corner of the room. He couldn't help feeling like a juggler who was being thrown extra balls. He had been able to adjust to the new business challenges up until now, but it was getting harder. How long before he dropped the balls altogether? "What are you going to do?"

Laura smiled. "I'll figure something out, just like you will with the Board of Directors meeting." She stood to leave, then turned back. "Hey, are we still on for dinner at your place tomorrow night?"

"Yeah. I figure it's probably up to us to keep these family get-togethers going . . . now that Mom isn't around to remind us. It's not like Scott and Brigitte are going to make the effort."

Laura laughed. "Unless we meet in a strip club. I bet Scott could get behind a sibling dinner at The Blue Room."

"Oh, come on. He's not that bad," Jack replied, but if he was being honest with himself, he wasn't so sure. Unpredictability was the one thing you could count on in his brother.

"I don't know. Maybe I misunderstood the guys in IT. . . But Brig is not much better."

"What? Brigitte wouldn't be caught dead in a place like that."

"No, not strip clubs. It's more like a lack of personal responsibility. I think her spending is getting out of control again. Do you know she just bought a Porsche? And this, after renting that huge downtown loft."

"I don't know what she's thinking. That place must be costing her a fortune. I know she's not getting paid enough for her rent *and* a Porsche payment. She's doing a great job in Promotions, but even a raise wouldn't be enough to keep her in that lifestyle."

"You know Brigitte—always thinking ahead. She's probably counting on her inheritance to cover her expenses," Laura said.

"The inheritance will be mostly stock. She can't pay rent and a car payment with stock certificates."

"That's true. I'm not sure what she's thinking. Mom isn't around to bail her out when things start to fall apart. I hope she knows what she's doing."

Jack rolled his eyes and pressed his hands to his temples. He didn't have time for Brigitte's drama today. Or ever, really. Just one more of the many things Meg had seemed to handle effortlessly that now appeared to be his responsibility.

"I'll see you at the meeting, then." Jack nodded and Laura left, closing the door behind her.

Was it too much to hope that Margaret McCallister's death would have finally been the thing to snap Scott and Brigitte out of their perpetual adolescence? If it didn't, Jack didn't know what would.

* * *

Jack took a seat at the conference table, most of his executive team seated around him. Marcia was tapping away at her tablet, her red fingernails clicking against the screen, while Walt pulled his fingers through the little grey hair he had left and opened up his laptop. Leslie Newell sat across the table, eyes glued to her smart phone, alternately scrolling and tapping through what Jack hoped were her sales team's numbers. Her sharp, black bob fell forward like a curtain, blocking her face from the rest of the room. Chris Lopez, Production Manager, came rushing through the door, slightly winded from his dash from the production floor. He landed in his chair with a huff and let an armload of clipboards and spreadsheets spill onto the table in front of him.

"Sorry I'm late," Chris said, his agitation written in his creased brow. "It's crazy down there. Switching gears halfway through the Grocery King order has us running around like chickens with our heads cut off."

Jack opened the meeting. "I appreciate you all being here. I know things are busy right now and your time is limited, so I'll get right to the point.

"It's an exciting time for Mama Meg's. I know it's hard to appreciate it when you're in the middle of the chaos," Jack nodded towards Chris, "but we're growing faster than ever. I've been thinking about this for a while, but now that Meg is gone, I think it's time to create a vision for how we are going to take her—I mean *our*—company to the next level."

Jack looked around the table from Laura, at his right, and beyond her to the rest of his executive team. He'd worked with them all for years, but now saw them in a new light. These were the people who would help him lead Mama Meg's into the future. Regardless of how removed Meg had been from the company for the last few years, Jack had to admit, it still felt like she was leading the ship. He'd relied on her experience and her knack for knowing the market. He'd freely borrowed from her guts and determination when he felt unsure of a certain course. Even though he'd been handed the reins long ago, it wasn't until this moment that he felt completely in charge.

And so he was grateful for his team's combined experience, their loyalty. He knew that, together, they could do great things.

"I'm meeting with the Board of Directors this afternoon," Jack stated, "and profits for some reason have taken a downturn. I'm sure it's temporary, but I need to let the Board know we've got a strategy—that we have a plan to boost every aspect of this business as we scale. I want Mama Meg's brand to be synonymous with quality and to have the respect of our customers, and the entire industry. We will set the standard for every other cookie on the market."

Jack had been looking at the numbers, seeing the growth, and knew, long before his mother passed, that it was time to grow the company. New markets, new products, new marketing and advertising campaigns. It was time. But to do all of that, they needed money.

"We need to reduce production costs," Jack stated, nodding in Chris's direction. "We need to expand our sales into new markets," he declared, turning his attention to Leslie, and then to Marcia. "Let's think of new ways to build the brand, maybe focus our efforts on social media, create a buzz."

"My team has been working on a viral campaign that we think the target demographic will respond well to," Marcia said. "I've also got my team working up a new marketing plan designed to strengthen brand image."

"That's great. Can you get me a few preliminary details to bring to the Board this afternoon?"

"I'm sending it to you now," Marcia said, with a few taps to her tablet.

"Great. Leslie? What are your sales ideas? How can we take away some of the market share from Oven Love and grow our sales?"

"I think it's time to expand into the Midwestern states. I was looking at Marcia's market research and if we hire a couple sales reps and a few more sales people, we can get a foothold before Oven Love."

"A couple of sales reps and a few sales people will eat into our profits, Jack," Walt pronounced, adjusting himself in his chair so he sat a bit taller. "I think we need to be careful about spending too much right now."

"Sales are what brings in more money, Walt. Anything we spend hiring new people in sales is an investment in our bottom line," Leslie answered.

"Leslie's right," Jack stated, even though Walt didn't seem convinced. "Increased sales are just what we need right now. If we sell more cookies, and we are smart about our costs, the money will take care of itself." Jack felt the burden of responsibility that had been weighing on him all morning finally lift. He was surrounded by experts. Together they would make this happen. How could he not succeed?

"Chris," turning his attention to his Production Manager, "what can be done to reduce manufacturing costs? Laura says one of the biggest problems is incorrect forecasting. I think if you and Sales can find a good workaround to get better information that would help."

"I agree," Chris replied. "Leslie and I can meet separately to work that out. In the meantime, I have a few other ideas." Chris rifled through the papers in front of him. "I had someone in Finance run these numbers this morning." He reached across the table to hand Jack a copy and pointed out places where he could trim expenses.

As Chris talked, Jack's confidence grew. A downturn in profits was surely temporary. The Board would see that. And once he outlined his vision for Mama Meg's growth, maybe the Board wouldn't be worried about profits.

Jack imagined what his mom's advice would be about all of this, but quickly remembered she was no longer around to give it. He didn't let this momentary melancholy dampen his confidence.

"I think we need to consider getting some organic products into R&D," Laura said. "I was talking to some of the sales people last week, and the market is practically begging for that stuff right now."

Leslie chimed in, "That's absolutely true. When I talk to our customers they all say that organic is the biggest area of growth for them."

"We'd have to have dedicated equipment to run that kind of product. That wouldn't be cheap," Jack stated.

"That's why I thought we could look at acquiring a smaller company," Laura added. "We'd have the production capacity for our new lines, as well as expand our market."

"Jack," Walt said, "I like the idea of cost-cutting measures in manufacturing, and I'm willing to concede that bringing on more sales people and expanding our territories are probably smart moves. But I don't think now is the time for acquisition. We simply don't have the money."

"Let me worry about that, Walt. Once we have more concrete plans, we can talk to the bank about a loan. If we don't keep up with new products, we run the risk of becoming irrelevant. I think we should move forward with organics." Then, turning to the rest of his executive team, he spoke, "I'll need detailed proposals from each of you about the things we talked about by next week. And Leslie?"

She looked up from her phone where she'd been taking notes.

"I'd like you to come with me to the board meeting this afternoon to address increasing our sales territories."

Leslie nodded.

As the meeting wrapped up, Jack watched his executive team file out of the room. He felt like he was on the right track to get Mama Meg's back in the black. The Board would see that and surely give him the go-ahead.

Laura lingered behind. After everyone had left, she said, "John Linde called, right before the meeting—about Mom's will."

John, the company and family attorney, had been with Margaret and Mama Meg's almost from the beginning. His value wasn't just in the way he understood Mama Meg's unique business needs, but his knowledge of the McCallister family dynamic.

"What about it? I thought it was pretty cut and dried. Everything is getting split evenly between the four of us, right?"

"It looks like Mom made a few changes that she didn't tell us about. You and I are ending up with more stock than Scott and Brig. About ten percent more." Laura looked at Jack, gauging his reaction.

"Okay, well, we have bigger roles—more responsibility in the company. Maybe that's why."

"John said it's because, over the years, Mom had to bail out Scott and Brig so many times. I guess she took that into consideration when splitting up her stock." Laura didn't bother hiding her concern. "You know, they are not going to be happy about this."

Jack exhaled, his irritation audible. Was he really going to have to parent these two grown siblings? When would they grow up? "Well, they're going to have to deal with it. Do they know?"

"John was going to call them as soon as he got off the phone with me."

He shook his head. "I can't do anything about Mom's will, and I've got to get ready for the board meeting. If they're going to throw a fit about it, let them. They'll get over it."

"I'll give them a call, see what they're thinking. Just get through the meeting and let me worry about those two," Laura responded.

"Fine. In the meantime, if you happen to know of any way I can make a downturn in profits sound like a good thing, let me know."

"Oh, you know the old trick," Laura said, patting Jack on the shoulder, the corners of her mouth inching up into a smirk. "Just flip that graph upside down and suddenly all our problems are fixed."

Jack smiled for the first time that day. Laura's ability to joke had always balanced out his tendency to worry. Family or not, Jack wouldn't have wanted anyone else as COO. No matter what happened, it was good to know that she had his back.

"If only it were that easy," Jack responded.

* * *

"I still don't see how you plan to turn things around," one of the board members demanded. "Right now, all you have are ideas. I need to know how you plan to execute."

"We would like to get new products into R&D. Specifically, organic cookies," Jack offered. "The market for those products is hot right now and our market research shows only getting hotter. I've got my executive team looking into it now."

"Until you've got costs under control, adding new products will just make your problems bigger," another board member dissented. "However, I agree that expanding your sales territories will get you a foothold in markets before your competition."

"Oven Love is killing us right now," Leslie spoke up from the back of the room. "They're just about ready to launch a new line of organic cookies. Mama Meg's needs to step up and compete with that. Without new product, our sales efforts won't be as effective."

Jack scanned the room as several of the board members broke off into discussions over the viability of the health food market. Two others, Gayle and Phil, had been quietly taking notes and had so far not had any input. Occasionally, one of them would point out something he or she had written and the other would nod and whisper.

Allen Paulson, Jack's friend and mentor, sitting as Chairman of the Board, was also observing more than he was talking for this meeting. Something seemed off. Finally, Allen spoke up, "The health food market is definitely a pie Mama Meg's should have a piece of. A large piece. But right now, you don't have the infrastructure to produce the product. Sales would love this product and would have no problem selling it. But if you can't deliver, you've lost more than profits."

"What do you suggest we do?" Jack asked.

"I'm not sure, but it seems like struggling profits could be a symptom of a bigger problem. Have you looked into that possibility?"

How had this meeting turned into a discussion about profits when he had such a strong vision for growth? He fought the feeling that he was on trial and tried to focus. "I'm confident that if we come up with a solid strategy, profits will respond positively. We're just experiencing growing pains. We've had them before and everything has always turned out fine. I don't see why this time would be any different." Why couldn't Allen see that?

"I know it makes sense on paper," Allen said, "but I think you need to go a different direction with your spending right now. Instead of investing in bigger territories, more products or acquisition, I think you need to look at your infrastructure—make sure you are ready to handle the increased business before bringing it on."

How could Allen say that? Mama Meg's didn't have time to sit back and watch Oven Love or anyone else pass them by. Now was the time to be aggressive.

Jack looked at Allen, who was waiting to see what he thought of the suggestion. Maybe he could buy himself another month, he thought. He could at least have someone look into efficiencies while they worked on fine-tuning their strategies for sales, marketing, manufacturing, and acquisition. It could buy him another month with the Board.

"We'll look into that, Allen. I'll get someone on that by the end of the day."

Allen looked satisfied. "Does anyone else have any suggestions for Jack?" Allen asked. The room fell silent as board members looked from side to side to see if anyone dared make the meeting run even one minute longer.

"Actually, Gayle and I have a suggestion," Phil declared, finally speaking up. The closing of laptops and shuffling of papers came to a halt and several people checked their watches but reluctantly turned their attention to the two board members.

"We think Mama Meg's has reached its peak with Jack at the helm. Over the last five years he brought this company even farther than Margaret could have—God rest her soul." He paused and looked at Gayle, who was nervously twitching her pen and looking at the table. Margaret had loaned Gayle the money to start her own business years ago and had supported and mentored her through her own company's successful growth. "Gayle?" Phil said, looking her way.

She cleared her throat, plainly nervous. "We think all the signs point to this being the perfect time to sell Mama Meg's."

Jack was sure he'd misheard her, but as the members of the Board and Leslie started to react with low mumbling and shifting in their seats, his gut quickly caught up with what his mind already knew, and understanding set in. She had actually just suggested selling Mama Meg's.

How had things turned so quickly? And how could Gayle get behind something like this? She never would have done this if Margaret had been alive.

She continued with a little more confidence despite the growing clamor of voices, "Oven Love has made an offer to buy Mama Meg's and we think the Board should take it seriously. If things continue the way they're going, this company will only lose value. Now is the time to sell if we want maximum profit."

"What?" Jack exclaimed and the room erupted with a burst of commotion.

"Hold on!" Allen cautioned. "Let's just hold on." He waited for the room to quiet, then said, "It doesn't matter how much Oven Love has offered. We'd have to have a majority of board members in agreement to move forward. We don't have a majority, do we?"

For a moment, no one moved. Jack felt the silence in the room was heavy and suffocating, like a lead blanket. He looked around the table. No one would meet his eye. Finally, Phil spoke. "I move for a vote."

"Fine," Allen said.

Jack had to be dreaming. Sure, things were a little tight right now, but they would turn around. Things had always worked out. He was not ready to lose Mama Meg's.

"All in favor of considering the offer to sell Mama Meg's to Oven Love . . ." Allen asked with authority.

Phil's hand went up, followed by Gayle's as she finally looked at Jack with an unspoken apology. Jack realized he'd been holding his breath. Maybe Phil and Gayle were the only ones in favor of selling. Maybe he had nothing to worry about. He slowly started to exhale when another hand slowly rose, and then another.

Allen scanned the room. "Is that everyone?" He paused to make sure, then said, "Just short of majority. Mama Meg's stays with the McCallister family for now."

"Not so fast, Allen," Phil retorted. "Majority shareholders have a vote in this decision too. That means the McCallister family."

Finally, a ray of hope, Jack thought. He knew Laura felt the same way he did about Mama Meg's. It was their mother's legacy and they were both committed to it. "There is no way Laura and I would consider selling to Oven Love. The family votes no."

"The family," Phil stated, "is more than just you and Laura, Jack."

Jack felt the bottom fall out from underneath him when he realized what Phil was implying. They wouldn't . . .

"Scott and Brigitte are in favor of selling Mama Meg's," Phil stated. "One more board member is all we need for a majority." Phil had the audacity to look smug, the bastard. "I'm sure in the coming months you will see that selling is the right decision." He directed his comments to the board members in favor of keeping Mama Meg's, but then turned to Jack and said, "It's not the end of the world, you know. Companies buy and sell each other all the time."

"You're not proposing a sale, Phil, and you know it. This is a takeover."

"The way I see it, it's an opportunity."

"Mama Meg's is not for sale. Period." Jack felt his face growing hot. He didn't want to lose control here, in front of the Board of Directors. He clenched his fists and took a deep breath. "I just need a little more time. Mama Meg's still has a lot of room to grow and I can get us there." Jack stood firm in front of the Board despite the tiny cracks he felt tearing into his confidence.

"Well, Jack," Phil said. "You don't have much time."

2

Parrying over a Pot Roast

The smell of pot roast hit Jack like an old friend the moment he walked into his home. But today, even those comforting memories of relaxed Sundays with the family weren't enough to erase the anger and sense of betrayal that had settled on him like a lead blanket. He came into the kitchen to find his ten-year-old son, Jason, digging through the silverware drawer.

"Hey, kiddo, is Mom around?" Jack asked, hiding the pain he was feeling.

"She's upstairs. She told me I had to set the table for dinner," Jason huffed, looking up at Jack as if he alone was the one who could rectify this great injustice. "Do we have to have Uncle Scott and Aunts Brigitte and Laura over for dinner?"

"Of course we do. You love your aunts and uncle. Why wouldn't you want them to come over?" Jack reached into the drawer and counted out forks, looking for anything to distract him.

"Mom always makes me sit at the kid's table," he fumed.

Jack pulled down seven glasses and started reaching for the plates. "Well, we don't have enough room at the big table. Who would you suggest sit at the kids' table in your place?"

"Uncle Scott acts like a kid. Make him sit there and drink out of tiny cups and eat off baby plates and listen to Allyson talk about dolls and dumb stuff like that."

"Well, I can fix your plate and cup situation," Jack said with a smile, handing his son a big plate and a tall glass, "but I'm afraid you are stuck with Allyson for now."

"You made it home just in time."

Jack turned to see his wife, Meredith, coming into the kitchen. "Yeah. I guess I'm a little late. Things took a crazy turn at work today."

"Good crazy, or bad crazy?" she asked.

Jack shook his head as a silent answer to her question, looked over at Jason, still setting the table, and motioned towards the office, where they could talk privately.

"Hey," Jason exclaimed, halting his half-hearted attempt at positioning folded napkins under forks, "I want to hear what happened at work today, too. I'm old enough."

"Finish setting the table," Meredith answered.

"This is so unfair," Jason whined, his voice fading away as they shut the office door.

As Jack filled Meredith in on the details of the board meeting, Gayle and Phil's suggestion that Mama Meg's should be sold, and Scott and Brigitte's surprise involvement and support of the idea, he felt his initial shock settle into a simmering anger. Scott and Brigitte's selfishness might actually put an end to his mother's legacy—the company killed by her own children. After his mother's hard work and sacrifice to build a company and raise a family, this felt like the ultimate betrayal. He didn't know how he would make it through a meal with those two without blowing up. Meredith suggested he let off some steam by mashing the potatoes.

"I thought you were going to suggest a beer and a foot rub?" Jack said, only half joking.

"Start mashing. I'll get you the beer, but the foot rub will have to wait for later."

Dinner went well, despite Scott's fart joke that made Jason snort milk out of his nose. Jack made a mental note to seat Scott at the kids' table next time. If there was a next time.

"You know I met with the Board this afternoon," Jack began, once Meredith excused herself to help the kids get ready for bed. He laid his napkin on the table beside his plate with a carefulness that countered the roil of emotions he was trying to keep from bursting out.

"We're aware," Scott retorted, answering for Brigitte, who seemed to suddenly find something fascinating in her lap to study.

Jack was too tired to be diplomatic. "Scott, Brig. What could you possibly be thinking? Going behind my back to try and sell Mama Meg's? And to Oven Love! Why didn't you come to me first?"

"As if you would have listened to our concerns? I know a waste of time when I see it," Scott countered.

"Waste of time?" Jack threw up his hands. "I guess you'd know. For the last ten years you've been conducting a thorough, hands-on study of the subject."

"Well, we can't all be CEO, can we?" Scott glared at Jack.

"See? This is exactly why we didn't want to say anything to you first, Jack," Brigitte exclaimed.

"Okay," Laura quickly interjected, trying to salvage the conversation, and the quickly devolving sibling relationships. "Why don't you tell us now? We'll listen with open minds, won't we, Jack?"

Jack nodded, even though he felt more like yelling than listening. "I'll hear you out."

"I'll just come out and say it. I want the money. We both do," declared Scott, inclining his head towards Brigitte. "This corporate life isn't for me. I'm not going to waste my life doing grunt work in some second-rate IT department."

"Maybe if you hadn't dropped out of college your freshman year to backpack through Europe you would have had a few more career options. You're the only one in IT that doesn't have at least a two-year degree. Gordon only agreed to hire and train you because Mom vouched for you." Jack replied.

"You don't have to remind me, brother," Scott snapped, spitting out the last word. "A scarlet letter would have drawn less attention to my social standing in IT. Twenty-two-year-old new-hires get more respect than I do."

"If you'd just made the smallest effort . . ." Jack countered.

"I stuck it out while Mom was alive, but I'm done now. I want out of this company and I want what Mom left me."

"Brig, what about you?" Laura asked. "I thought you liked working in Promotions."

"I like my job. I don't want to quit. But I do want my money. It's only fair. Why should I have to wait?"

"You realize you will probably be let go if we are bought out by Oven Love," Laura pointed out.

"I can get another job." Brigitte waved her hand as if swatting away a tiny bug. "But I might not have another opportunity to have my loft apartment featured in *Dwell*. I can't pass that up."

"*Dwell*?" Laura asked. The strain to make the connection etched lines across her forehead.

"The Urban Lifestyles editor called. Well, it was her assistant. Or assistant's assistant. Anyway, he said that a Jan Showers-designed living space is exactly the kind of thing their magazine would love to feature," Brigitte said, pride dripping off each word.

"You don't have a 'Jan Showers-designed living space,'" Laura replied.

"But I could," Brigitte retorted, "with the money that Mom left me."

"So you're willing to trade in Mama Meg's for new furniture?" Jack said with frustration. He couldn't believe the fate of his mother's company could be decided over something as stupid as an ottoman and a few throw pillows. Could Brigitte even hear herself talking?

"I guess you could say we're just not as attached to the company as you and Laura are, Jack. Brig and I aren't interested in wasting our lives in dead-end jobs only to get a hunk of cash when we are too old to enjoy it. And you know, Jack," Scott continued, "Gayle thinks this is the perfect time to sell. She and Mom were good friends. I don't think Gayle would get behind this if she didn't think it was a good idea."

"Gayle's an idiot," Jack grumbled into his napkin.

"Surely you could wait a few years for the money," Laura suggested. "We don't need to sell now. Maybe if we waited five years, we could look at selling again. Mama Meg's would be worth more then."

"No way," Scott declared. "Phil and Gayle think the company's going to *lose* value, not gain it. And since Mom so kindly had the will changed to benefit her two favorites . . ."

"Now wait a second," Laura said, clearly unable to keep up her façade of calm one second longer. "You talked to John today. You know exactly why the stock was portioned out the way it was. Do I need to spell it out for you, Mr. I've-Run-Out-of-Money-And-I'm-Stuck-in-Naples?" Jack knew by the rise in her voice and the sudden stiffening of her spine that she was done playing the self-appointed peacemaker.

"And what about the BMW you bought on your lunch hour, Brig? You paid sticker without even negotiating. And when you were upside down on your loan and couldn't afford the payments, who bailed you out? Mom!" She turned to her younger brother. "And Scott," she continued, "do the words 'solar lenses' ring a bell? Remember taking the tax credit but never actually paying for the lenses? Who came to your rescue when the IRS was banging down your door? Mom! That's who! You two have had your extra ten percent of stock and then some."

Now Jack stepped in to pull the conversation back from the edge to some form of civility. "Clearly this is something we aren't going to agree on tonight." He spread his hands out on the table as if the gesture itself would hold things together.

Laura sat back in her chair, crossed her arms in defiance and glared. Scott and Brigitte had the audacity to look smug. Could it be they were doing this for revenge—because Meg had left them less in the will? Jack wouldn't put that kind of behavior past Scott, but he couldn't believe Brigitte's motives would be so vicious.

"Let us talk to John Linde and get some advice. Maybe we can buy your shares and we won't have to sell the company." Jack knew their long-time family friend and attorney would find a way to keep Mama Meg's from a hostile takeover if he could, but he noticed Scott didn't look convinced.

"I'll give you a few days," Scott agreed, "but we want what's ours. If you can't figure out how to give it to us, we'll push for the sale of Mama Meg's to Oven Love. And it won't take long to convince a few other people on the Board to vote our way."

Jack wasn't sure what he was going to do, but he knew he had to look at every possibility before giving up. Keeping Mama Meg's in the family was important to him, but if he was honest, so was putting Scott in his place. He wouldn't let an aimless screw-up have this much power over what happened to his mother's company.

"Jack," Laura said, after Scott and Brigitte had left, "I know finding a way to placate those two seems like the biggest problem on your plate right now, but we can't set aside the your vision for the company. After our team meeting today, we have some momentum, and a stronger Mama Meg's will only help our cause."

Jack nodded in agreement. "The executive team needs to know what is going on—to understand how urgent it is that we grow the company and improve our position in our market. I won't lose focus of that. I'll just have to trust that John can work something out that will appease them."

"He better also come up with something we can actually do," Laura added. "Do you really think we are in a position to buy them out?"

"I know we're not—at least not right now."

"John won't let us go down without a fight." Laura stated. If anyone had as much emotionally invested in Mama Meg's as they did, it was John, who'd been with them from the first 500-square-foot, hole-in-the-wall bakery to the 15,000-square-foot facility they operated in today. Margaret and John had been such close friends, Jack had often wondered if there was something more than just business to their relationship. If there was, his mom never said anything about it.

"Now, about developing your vision," Laura continued, "why don't we take the team off site? We need strategies that will work, and we need them quickly. A focused day with the team together would be a great way to pound out a plan."

Jack knew she was right but still questioned himself. *What would Mom do?* He wondered. Even though all he wanted to do was sit down with John and find a solution to get Scott and Brigitte off his back and pacify the Board, he knew his time was better spent developing strategies to make Mama Meg's stronger.

So he called a meeting.

* * *

The hotel wasn't fancy, but it had a conference room and was available on short notice, which was all Jack needed. The topic of discussion for the morning was sales. Leslie was already in the conference room with two of her sales managers and her assistant when Jack entered. They were going over sales data when the rest of the executive team filed in.

Laura and Chris took seats next to Walt while Marcia got a cup of coffee and a bagel from the tray of food the hotel had provided.

"You may have already heard," Jack stated, "that several members of the Board of Directors think we should sell Mama Meg's." Jack scanned the room. He had everyone's attention now. By the looks on everyone's faces, it seemed like Leslie had actually kept her mouth shut after yesterday's meeting. "Unfortunately, my brother Scott and my sister Brigitte are in favor of the sale and are aggressively pushing for it. To make matters worse," Jack now watched his team carefully as he delivered the final piece of bad news, "Oven Love has made an offer to buy."

Marcia let out an audible gasp and Walt sank his head into his hands. Chris looked from side to side as if trying to verify what he had just heard with those sitting near him. Leslie, on the other hand, hardly reacted at all. She stared blankly, not meeting Jack's eyes. Of course she'd already known about the takeover bid from her attendance at the meeting, but there was something about her stoicism that seemed off.

"Do we have a timeline?" Marcia asked.

"Are they close to a majority? How many more votes do they need?" Chris inquired.

"Jack," Walt said, the sharp tone of his voice not masking his unease, "please tell me you and Laura are going to fight this."

"That's exactly why we're here today," Jack replied. "Laura and I are totally committed to keeping Mama Meg's in the family for a long time. I've got John Linde working on a way to satisfy Scott and Brigitte and to buy us some time. But we need to move forward with strategies to grow this company. We need some solid plans."

"Jack's right," Laura added. "A stronger Mama Meg's is in a better position to come out on top. It's about more than just getting through this buyout threat. We've got to have more value, more negotiating power and more of a reason not to sell to Oven Love."

Jack nodded his agreement. "So, the stakes just got a little higher. It's no longer only about raising profits. What we decide to do today may be what saves the company."

Walt nodded and Marcia did, too. Chris looked thoughtfully at the ceiling as if expecting answers, or maybe divine help. At this point, Jack was open to all the help they could get. Leslie was dispassionately swiping and tapping away on her phone. Did she even care that Oven Love was threatening a takeover? Jack shook his head as if to clear it. Of course she did. Of all the people on his executive team, Leslie and Meg had seemed to have a special connection. They shared a certain boldness and audacity that served them well in their careers. Leslie had considered Meg not only a mentor, but a friend.

"In our last meeting, we talked about expanding sales territories," Jack said, deciding not to worry about her loyalty for now. "Leslie, what information do you have for us?"

Leslie laid out her plans to expand into Midwest markets while Marcia backed her up with demographic data. Leslie had prepared well and it became clear that this expansion had been something she'd been thinking about for a while. "With increased sales from our new areas, we could increase Mama Meg's revenue by up to ten percent."

"What do you need from each of us to make this successful?" Jack asked.

"I'm going to need new product samples so we can get them out to our customers," she said, while Laura made notes. "Three new sales people and a regional sales manager." Leslie paused, then added, "and a Customer Relationship Management system so we can streamline flow. No more lags in communication or lack of information. Most importantly," Leslie turned to Laura, "my sales forecasts would be accurate. You'll be able to make informed purchasing decisions and save money and time from having to buy ingredients at jacked-up prices and shut down lines while you wait for them to arrive."

"I see no way a CRM system would fit into the current budget," Walt cautioned. "We can justify hiring sales people, but ultimately, profits are still in a downturn. This is not the time for indiscriminate spending."

"Well, maybe we need to reallocate some of the budget, because right now, we are losing money because of slow turnaround times, ingredient shortages and factory shutdowns. It takes my people weeks to close a sale," Leslie explained. "They have to return to the office, check inventory and orders in queue, then get back with the customer and just hope Oven Love hasn't beaten us to the sale in the meantime. If inventory numbers were more accurate," she turned to Chris, almost accusingly, "my sales forecasts would reflect that. My forecast is just a guess because that's the best I can do with the data I have to work with."

Walt spoke up again. "I have more issues with Leslie's plan than just an expensive computer program," he said, taking control of the conversation. "You claim that opening a new area will increase revenue. That is probably true, but right now, we can't pinpoint exactly what our profits will be on any one product. We have no idea which ones are making us the most money, and which ones are losing."

"Why can't we figure that out?" Jack probed. "We know exactly what we are spending on raw materials, and we know what our overall profits are each month."

"Can't we just look at our inventory and production numbers to figure that out?" Leslie asked.

"That doesn't tell us the whole story," Walt explained. "To get accurate numbers, we need to know exactly what percentage of our total raw materials went into each product."

"Also, when we buy on the spot market," put in Laura, "the final cost of the cookie is going up, but our price stays the same and the profit goes down. And we have no idea exactly how much."

"Add in the cost of having to break down a line because we are out of ingredients," Chris chimed in. "Not only is that inefficient—we're constantly late getting orders filled for Leslie's customers—I have to pay my guys to stand around while we wait for everything to get up and running again. That waste isn't even part of our current equation."

"Well, it needs to be," Walt said, closing his eyes in concentration and tapping his finger to his lips as if to drum out a solution. "A CRM system might make your team more efficient, but it's not going to solve all our other problems."

"I agree," Chris stated, looking at Laura, then back at Walt.

"Our current inventory spreadsheet should have the information we need to create an accurate product profitability matrix," Walt said.

"I've got that spreadsheet pinned up in my office and it covers one whole wall," Chris complained. "Gives me a headache to look at it too long. The numbers start swimming and then . . ." Chris rubbed his temples at the thought. "Please don't make a bigger spreadsheet."

"If I do an inventory overhaul—find out what we have in terms of available stock, how much we are spending on raw materials, the depreciation on our equipment—we should be able to come up with pretty accurate information that gives us a good idea of our most profitable products," Walt offered. "I'll have my purchasing department come up with a weekly report and we can add that information into the spreadsheet."

Chris started rubbing his temples again and let out a soft moan.

"It'll work, Chris." There was encouragement in Walt's voice and years of experience behind his idea. "If you can help me out with the inventory numbers, I should have an updated spreadsheet with our profitability in a couple weeks. That will actually help us all." Walt sat back in his chair and looked around the table at each person as if to gauge their response. "But the organic product profitability will be more difficult to project. We'll be dealing with ingredients we've never purchased before. Quantities, price—these are unknowns."

"I can work with R&D to get some projections to you," Laura offered.

"This will help us know which products we should focus on selling, but if those products aren't in the warehouse, or there are no ingredients to make them, my guys are going to lose customers when they can't deliver," Leslie cautioned, jabbing her finger into the table to emphasize her point.

"Is there any way to get better access to inventory numbers?" Jack asked.

"Not unless Chris has a better way to track the jobs on the production line," Leslie replied.

"I've got my people working their asses off, but I don't know if there is anything more I can do without a better way to track what we're using," Chris said.

"If we are going to kick Oven Love's butt, Sales needs the right tools. We need fast access to data about what's in inventory and what's queued up for production." Leslie declared.

"What about speeding up the data coming out of Production? Chris? Is there any way your team can streamline the way you get your numbers over to Leslie?" Jack asked.

"If we had a way to track procurement," Chris explained, "raw materials, inventory, finished goods . . . I could run much more efficiently with that kind of data at hand. That would definitely help with information flow."

"I thought we had someone tracking all those numbers on a spreadsheet. Walt?" Jack asked, looking for confirmation.

"That would be Alice in Accounts. She can run you any kind of report you need, Chris. She's pretty quick, too. Couple of hours is usually all it takes if she's not busy with other work," Walt said with confidence and finality, as if this solution would finally satisfy Chris.

Chris dropped his head into his hands and let out a sigh of exasperation, then, just as quickly, raised his head and looked at Jack. "I don't have a couple hours to wait for a report and I don't need twenty more sheets of paper to add to this pile," he said, shoving the stack in front of him to fan across the table. "With the amount of product we're running, I need to make decisions faster than that."

"Chris makes a good point," Laura agreed. "If Production doesn't have the right data at the right time, we can't accurately set up lines. We end up running out of ingredients before an order is completed. It may not sound like that big of a deal, but when that happens, we don't just have a few hours of down time. We are losing days, and that has a huge effect on our bottom line. Of all people, you should be able to understand that, Walt."

Walt's brows knit in concern. "What takes so long to change out a product line?"

Chris spoke up. "Whenever we have to change lines for new products, we have to do everything manually. We have our recipes in one system, but production control is in another. Someone has to sit down and enter all that data back into production systems so we get the right recipe and ingredients together in the production line."

"So the recipe data and the inventory data aren't integrated?" Walt asked.

Chris and Laura shook their heads.

Walt leaned back in his chair and swiveled around to face Jack, his yellow bow-tie rising and falling as he took a breath, then exhaled. "All the information we need is on the spreadsheets.

Yes, it takes a little time to get them updated, but the system is solid, as long as we get good input of information."

"It just feels like the spreadsheets aren't working anymore, Walt. Like we've outgrown them." Laura stated. "We are having to make decisions faster than we're getting information, and many times, we're making the wrong ones because of it."

Jack felt like the conversation was getting off track. They'd veered from their agenda and he worried about having enough time to cover everything he wanted. Still, he squashed the urge to bring the conversation back around to their sales vision. Something told Jack their information problem had more to do with sales, and ultimately, every aspect of his vision.

Could more spreadsheets fix the problems they were having? Jack hoped they would.

After a quick lunch break, they got right back to work. Walt began by explaining the hurdles they would have to overcome if they were to make an acquisition.

"I understand the importance of keeping up with the market trends, but I just want you to know what this will entail." Walt showed some slides of graphs and spreadsheets to make his point. "It's not impossible," he explained, "but it will be difficult with our current financial situation."

Despite the less than enthusiastic delivery, Jack had always admired the way Walt had been able to bring things into perspective, and assure him, with numbers, that all was well. He never used exuberance or whimsy to make a point. He didn't need to. His data always spoke for itself.

"I've got my team working on a plan," Walt continued. "We need to make sure that the money is in place and that the organic products will actually be profitable before moving forward, but I'll work with R&D to answer those questions. And I'll talk to the bank as well. Along with working with Chris on the product profitability matrix, I think I should also change up the way I'm getting information out to everyone. It makes sense that as the company grows, though, we will need to adjust the way we are doing things." Walt spoke with authority. "It's possible we need a dedicated team for each department to handle gathering information and distributing it."

And with that, they were back to talking about spreadsheets.

"My concern is that there could be errors in the data," Chris put in. "It's happened before and it's caused us to over- or under-purchase supplies, neither of which are efficient ways to run my department."

"If I can't get the information instantly," added Leslie, "it won't do me much good. I've got people in the field whose sales depend on having production numbers at their fingertips. When there are work stoppages because you've run out of ingredients before the order is finished, it almost always means my sales people have to smooth things over with the customer."

"It is obvious that access to accurate and timely spreadsheets is going to help everyone run their departments better," Walt said. "I'll make some phone calls this afternoon and have my team come up with a plan to streamline the way everyone is getting their data. We will have it in place by the first of next week." Walt's concern was genuine. "If we don't see marked improvements, we can explore other options," he offered.

"We do need a quick fix to this problem," Laura agreed. "I think we should go forward with Walt's plan."

"Let's do it," Chris agreed, leaning back in his chair and rubbing his temples again, submitting to the sub-optimal solution.

"I'm not sure this is going to make one bit of difference," Leslie countered. "The only real way for me to run my department efficiently is with a CRM system. At this point, the spreadsheets are a Band-Aid on a gushing wound."

"I agree that we will need to address the information flow more aggressively, Leslie," Jack said, "but right now, a quick fix is exactly what we need. We've got to hold off this takeover and get profits moving in the right direction. Once those things are taken care of, we will have time to focus on long-term solutions, like a CRM system. Are there any other ideas?" he asked, and then, seeing Leslie roll her eyes, said, "Besides Leslie?" When no one raised any other objections, Jack went on, "Okay. Let's move off the subject of the spreadsheets and on to the other items on our agenda. Walt, follow up with me by the end of the week on your plan."

They continued to work through dinner and finally wrapped things up around 9:30. Jack was exhausted, but exhilarated at the same time. Still, he knew that if giving each department a dedicated person to handle their spreadsheets didn't work, they were going to have to find another solution fast. Leslie's desire for a CRM was a good one. It just wasn't the right time. She hadn't been subtle with her displeasure at rejection, though, keeping quiet and sullen throughout the rest of the meeting, answering in short sentences. Jack knew she was stewing, but knew she'd come around in a day or two, once she saw that the spreadsheets could work. At least he *hoped* they would work.

"A few of us are heading out for drinks," Laura said, coming back to help Jack gather his things. "Want to join us? It's been a long day."

"Who's going?" Jack asked as he shuffled a pile of spreadsheets into a messy stack.

"Marcia, Chris, Leslie . . ."

Jack thought of the simmering grudge Leslie had held all day and figured the griping would only get louder and more obnoxious after a few drinks. "Thanks, but I'll pass," he said, not just because he was tired of Leslie. He was ready to go home and let someone else be the boss for a while.

3

Working on a Dull Blade

Jack woke early the next morning with thoughts from the previous day's meeting vying for room in his head. With a mix of excitement, energy and a touch of panic, he decided to skip his morning run and get right to work. By the time the first rays of sun were lighting the windows of his home office, he'd already responded to all of his email, looked over reports, and scheduled a meeting with Allen Paulson—who had just been finishing dinner in Shanghai—for the next week.

As he drove in to work, the one remaining cloud casting a shadow on his bright outlook was the question of how to appease Scott and Brigitte. John Linde was not an early riser and Jack had learned long ago that there was no use in trying to reach him before nine a.m. He would have to wait a little longer to find out what he'd come up with. He hated waiting.

As he pulled his Land Rover into his parking space, Laura's Prius slid in right beside him. Jack got out of his car and went over to meet Laura as she was getting out of hers.

"You seem unusually chipper this morning," she said, as if it was an accusation. She took a little longer than usual to get out of her car. Rising carefully from her seat, she slung her laptop bag over her shoulder and came around the car to join him. "How dare you?"

Jack chuckled. Laura's hair was pulled back into a ponytail, which told him all he needed to know about how late she'd been out last night. Of course the bags under her eyes were a big clue, too. "Late night?"

"I should have just gone home when you did," she groaned. "I'm never having another oyster shooter again."

"Oyster shooters? I thought you hated shellfish."

"My judgment was impaired."

"Well, I feel great." Jack passed through the lobby and to the stairs, taking them two at a time. He craned his neck to talk over his shoulder. "Of course, I would feel a little better if I knew how John's meeting with Scott and Brigitte went."

Laura was still at the bottom of the stairs, taking each step with the care of a poised professional, or someone who was trying very hard not to fall on her face. If Jack knew Laura, she probably thought she was pulling off the first scenario.

"If you say so." She finally reached the top of the stairs and Jack, who was waiting for her. "But I think you should know . . . Leslie was doing a lot of talking last night."

"Yeah? She piss off any biker gangs with her argument that Yamahas are better than Harleys?"

"No, I don't think she'll make that mistake again. Although, she did try to convince the bartender his vodka tasted like nail polish remover and he should stock a different brand."

Jack rolled his eyes.

"You'd have thought she was working on commission."

Jack unlocked the door to his office, opened it and walked in, flipping on the light behind him. Laura followed. "So, what about Leslie's big mouth?"

"For starters, she seemed very interested that all Oven Love's sales people just got that new CRM program, 'E-Sales Manager.'" Laura paused as she tried to stifle a gaping yawn.

"Of course she was. That's no surprise."

"I know, but last night it was almost like she was using it as an example of Oven Love's—I don't know—superiority; how they're in a better position than Mama Meg's. She knew a lot about products they still have in development."

"She's in sales. She has to be up on that stuff to be competitive."

Laura shook her head, setting her ponytail swinging, and then stopped suddenly, remembering her temporarily forgotten headache. "I'm not talking about general information. She knew stuff only a few in Oven Love's top level management would be privy to."

"So you think she's got a contact over there? Someone she might be trading information with?" asked Jack. His voice was in control, betraying almost none of the panic he felt. He couldn't fool Laura, though.

"Listen, I'm sure it's a misunderstanding. She'd had a few drinks . . . you know how she gets," she assured him. "Like you said, she's in sales. She has to know about these things to compete. Maybe you should talk to her—find out what she knows and maybe how."

"You think she'll just spill her secrets if she has something to hide?" Jack's eyes narrowed as he thought.

"I know she plays by her own set of rules, but Leslie's not a liar." Laura paused while Jack considered this. "Don't you trust her?"

"I don't know. I don't want to be blindsided, again. This thing with Scott and Brigitte—I never thought they'd betray us like this. I'm a little wary, that's all."

"Talk to her. Ask her what else she knows about Oven Love's motives . . . Where she's getting her information. Maybe something she knows can help us?"

"Alright," Jack said, checking his watch. It was after nine o'clock. "I've got to call John now. I'll worry about Leslie later." He sighed, any remaining energy from his productive morning seeping out through this latest puncture to his trust.

Before leaving, Laura said, "She's been with us for five years. That's got to mean something. I'm sure she's loyal to Mama Meg's." She pulled the door closed behind her, leaving Jack with a dim hope that she was right.

* * *

Jack sat at his desk, phone to his ear. "Please tell me you've got good news."

"Some good, some . . . not so good," John said, his warm voice a little creaky with age and experience, which Jack usually found comforting. But now there was a clear sense of foreboding when John spoke. "The good news?" he said, "Scott and Brigitte have agreed to a buyout."

"That's great." Jack felt like a weight had been lifted off his chest and he could breathe deeply for the first time since the board meeting last week. "How much time do we have to come up with the money?"

"We've agreed to one year."

"Okay. That's going to be tight, but not impossible." That wasn't so bad—certainly not bad enough to warrant John's gloomy tone. Maybe he was getting a little dramatic in his old age. Jack started doing quick calculations in his head, but coming up short each time. He was confident once he sat down with Walt, they'd be able to work out a plan.

"Actually, Jack, I've seen your numbers. I think 'tight' is a bit generous. A year isn't going to be enough."

"I'll work things out. If we reach a year and still aren't in a position to buy out those two, I'll cross that bridge when I come to it. You've bought me time, John. That's all I wanted. This is great news." Jack let out a low chuckle. "You had me worried, though. The way you were talking . . . I thought you had really bad news."

There was a long pause, then John said, "I haven't told you the bad part yet."

"You, what? What more could there be? Scott and Brig agreed to the buyout. I have a year. Done."

"In order to get the two of them to agree to the buyout, to wait a year, and to keep them from voting for the sale of Mama Meg's to Oven Love, Scott demanded a higher buyout price."

Jack felt the weight start to press down again. "How much."

When John told him the amount, Jack lowered his head to the desk and let the phone slide from his hand.

"Jack? You still there?"

Jack had to think about it for a few seconds, then, picking the phone back up, said, "Yeah. But I won't be for long, will I? There's no way we can meet their price."

"It does seem impossible," John agreed. "But you have a year. A lot can happen in a year."

John's words echoed in Jack's head after he said goodbye and hung up the phone. A lot *could* happen in a year. But what if he worked and worked and still had to sell to Oven Love in twelve months? For the briefest moment, he considered giving up. Agreeing to the takeover now and walking away from Mama Meg's, and Scott and Brigitte.

At the thought of his brother and sister, their betrayal and unbending demands, Jack felt anger rising in his chest, burning and determined. The demands might have come from both Brigitte and Scott, but he knew it was Scott driving this steamroller. Brigitte was simply a convenient passenger in his demolition derby. Jack wondered when he'd changed from a fun, spontaneous, good-natured brother to a selfish asshole who was doing his damnedest to take down his mother's fifty-million-dollar-a-year cookie company.

If Scott had been in the room, Jack would have punched him. After all their mother had done for him: the bailouts, the job, the money she'd been funneling into one failed scheme after the other for the last ten years. This is how Scott was repaying her? He didn't deserve anything.

Not for the first time, Jack wondered what his mother would do if Scott had tried to pull something like this while she was alive. He laughed at the thought and realized, the tongue-lashing she would have given him is exactly why he had waited until she was gone.

Could he get this company where it needed to be in a year on his own . . . without his mom's guidance? Jack wasn't sure he had it in him. But what he did know was that Scott couldn't win.

He beat back his lingering doubts that he was up to the task of running this company. He had to be. It was now or never.

* * *

At their weekly meeting, Jack watched as Chris rifled through his spreadsheets. "I've got that information right here . . ." He finally found what he was looking for and ran his finger down the column and stopped, jabbing the page. "We are losing twenty-one hours of production time, not including what we lose sending home salaried employees when we have a work stoppage."

"I need to know where things are breaking down," Jack said. "I know we've already gone over all of this. Leslie needs to get accurate sales data to Chris, but Production needs to give Sales a better idea of lead times and inventory. The data is getting into the spreadsheets, right, Walt?"

Walt nodded. "I've pulled four people off other jobs and, right now, they are dedicated to keeping each department updated. But they can only work as fast as they're getting the numbers. If that doesn't come in until the end of the day, the spreadsheets go out first thing the next morning."

"I can't believe we have to do all of this manually," Jack exclaimed. "Shouldn't we be able to pull those numbers off a shared system? We spent a ton of money on an Enterprise Resource Planning system that was supposed to take care of this for us. Why isn't it meeting those needs?" he asked. He turned to Walt. "Didn't we evaluate that system last year? I thought we were happy with the way it was working for us."

"Last year it was mostly Accounting that was using the program and they didn't have any issues. None of the other departments seemed to think it was particularly helpful," Walt said. "So we decided to keep it. New systems and their implementation are a huge expense and time commitment; we didn't see a need to take that on."

"We might need to reconsider that," Jack said, shaking his head. "It doesn't seem like the spreadsheets are working." Walt started to interject something, but Jack continued, "I know you've done everything you can, Walt, but there's a disconnect. We are losing money and it keeps coming back to the lack of timely, accurate information." Jack paused and looked around the room, waiting to see if anyone disagreed. Chris was nodding his head while Leslie shot Marcia a knowing look, as if to say, *Wasn't I just talking to you about this?*

"Any new system takes a while to work the bugs out," Walt insisted. "We need to give the spreadsheets a chance. We've only been doing this for a week. Once everyone gets used to using them, things will run much more smoothly."

"Is it possible for our current ERP system to take over any of these spreadsheets?" Jack inquired. "Maybe if we could get a report to Chris, or Laura, it would be easier and quicker for them to access. Then you wouldn't have to take so many people off other jobs to work on updating the data."

"The ERP system was always more of an accounting tool, as opposed to a materials requirement planning system," replied Walt. "There is a manufacturing module available, but it's expensive, and with the amount of business we were doing, we never needed it before."

"Maybe it's time to upgrade to a new ERP system," Jack said.

"It sounds like it might help Sales, too," Laura offered.

"I don't think that's a good idea, Jack." Walt shook his head. "Even if we had the money in the budget to spend on a new system, it will take months to transition. We need solutions that are going to help us now. We need solid strategies you can take to the Board to convince them to side with us and not Scott and Brigitte. Our time is better spent continuing to fine-tune and implement our plans we discussed at last week's off-site meeting."

"You're probably right," Jack admitted, his last encounter with the Board still stinging. "A big purchase doesn't seem to make sense when we're trying to increase our bottom line. We'll stick with the ERP system we've got now, and maybe next year we can determine if it's time for an upgrade." He looked around the table "How does everybody feel about that?"

Walt nodded. "Our ideas are good, Jack. The focus needs to be on how we are going to make everything happen. That's what the Board wants to hear. The spreadsheets will become more user-friendly once we get used to them."

"I'm not wild about it, but I'll make it work", said Chris. "I'm still not getting the information I need as fast as I need it, but it's better than what we've got now."

"We'll work at getting the information to production as fast as we can, but it won't be as quick as having a CRM system in place", Leslie said with a thin smile.

Jack left the meeting feeling unsettled. On paper, it made sense to hold off on a major purchase that would certainly disrupt the flow of business for who knew how long. But bigger and more detailed spreadsheets didn't seem to be cutting it anymore. With the spreadsheets, there were too many ways things could go wrong. And now, more than ever, he couldn't afford mistakes.

His mind was ricocheting between potential solutions to his problem, quite lost in his own thoughts, when he rounded the corner and nearly plowed right into someone coming the other direction.

"Jack. There you are." It was Allen Paulson. Jack pulled back, just in time to avoid the collision. Allen was around six-foot-three but bigger than life in reputation and Jack had respected him as long as he'd known him. Allen lived his life with the same passion with which he'd done business, summiting Mt. Everest about the same time his company was breaking into the Fortune 1000 list.

"Allen, good to see you." Jack attempted to downplay his initial surprise. He hadn't forgotten his appointment, but to say his mind was monopolized by other things was an understatement.

Luckily, Allen was diplomatic. "Trying to keep the company from crashing down around you?" Jack laughed darkly as Allen gestured towards Jack's office. "It's usually not as bad as it seems, you know."

"The key word being 'usually,'" returned Jack, holding the door open for Allen, then letting it swing shut behind him. Allen grabbed a seat and didn't bother with pleasantries.

"I hear your brother and sister are tightening the screws."

"That's one way to put it." Jack shifted in his chair, and then said, "The way I see it, it's going to take a miracle to buy them out. But I'll be damned if I'm going to sit by and not work my hardest to pull that miracle off." Jack paused as Allen nodded knowingly. "We're putting a plan in place right now, opening new sales territories, a new marketing strategy, planning acquisition, new product development—we're moving forward."

Jack rehashed all the details of the strategy his team had been working on for the last week and if Allen's thoughtful nods were any indication, he was on the right track.

"My team is all on board and invested in making this happen. It's just. . ." Jack trailed off.

Allen waited a beat, then said, "It's just what? What is the thing that is getting in the way of taking Mama Meg's to the next level?"

Jack got the distinct feeling Allen knew the answer to his own question, but wanted Jack to say it out loud. "We can't seem to get a handle on our data. Late and inaccurate information is slowing down production, negatively affecting sales, and frankly, draining our profits. We've got a team dedicated to updating and distributing spreadsheets to the different departments, but it's not enough. The spreadsheets are becoming unmanageable and clunky. But they're our only option right now. We just have to figure out a way to make them work."

"Listen," Allen said, "when you were a small company, the spreadsheets worked fine. But you've outgrown them. You can't keep relying on them if you want Mama Meg's to keep growing, and more importantly, if you want to buy out Scott and Brigitte."

"We can't afford a new system right now. I've talked about it with Walt and he agrees. It's too much money and will disrupt the flow of business until everyone learns how to use it. Any other time, I'd say yes. But with Scott and Brigitte breathing down my neck. . ."

"You know I sit on the board of SST Manufacturing and they're going through almost the exact same thing as Mama Meg's." Then he added as an afterthought, "Minus the brother and sister from Hell."

Jack let out a sardonic laugh. "Lucky them."

"Just like you, they've gotten to a point where their enterprise software systems weren't able to scale up to match the growth of their company. There comes a point where spreadsheets won't cut it anymore. They reached that point, and you have, too." Allen leaned back in his chair and stretched, resting his hands behind his head.

"So, what's their solution?"

"They brought in an Information Technology consultant. He did an evaluation of their company and came up with a set of recommendations that they immediately implemented. It's been about three months now and, it's still early, but things are starting to turn around."

"What do you mean, turn around?" Jack sat forward, leaning his arms on his desk.

"They've implemented an IT governance committee to examine and prioritize projects. They decide which projects will get the resources and which will be temporarily set aside. Not only can they move forward, knowing they're on the right track, it also provides buy-in from each department. No one has pet projects anymore—they're all working together for the same goal." Allen leaned back in his chair, smiling. "And that's the key, Jack. Everyone needs to be moving together towards the same goal."

"That sounds promising," Jack said. "But consultants are expensive. And their suggestions are surely going to cost us more money."

"You don't have the luxury of thinking in terms of money right now. You're at a point in Mama Meg's growth where you're standing in front of a huge cliff face. You have to figure out a way to get up that cliff and keep growing."

"What if we're not ready to make that leap? What if circumstances—my brother and sister, for example—make that move risky?" That was really the wrench in the machine. If it weren't for Scott's demands and a takeover by Oven Love hanging over his head, Allen's suggestion to bring on a consultant might make sense.

"You could stay where you are, but I can guarantee the result will be Mama Meg's gets sold to a company who knows how to scale the mountain."

Jack couldn't think of any response to that. The way Allen was talking, he didn't have many options.

"I think you should consider bringing this consultant in."

Jack closed his eyes and his head fell back against his chair as Walt's assurances about the spreadsheets and his own instinct went to the mat in what felt like the ultimate grudge match.

"You lose nothing by talking to this guy," Allen interjected, as if he could see the wrestling going on in Jack's head. He pushed a business card across the desk. "You said you needed a miracle? I think you should start off with a consultant."

Jack looked at the card. *Emmett Trask, Information Technology Consultant*, it read.

Allen pushed back his chair and stood up to leave. "Oh, and Jack? I told him to expect your call."

4

On Guard

Jack and Walt sat across the conference room table from Emmett Trask. His crisp blue shirt looked like it had never known a wrinkle and his pale, yellow tie seemed to say, *Relax*. His laptop was open, ready and eager like a Labrador Retriever waiting to hear a command.

After their phone conversation, Jack had felt better and better about his meeting with Emmett. It seemed clear that someone with a view from the outside was exactly what was needed to make good decisions. He knew his mom would have agreed. Jack couldn't even identify Mama Meg's problem let alone come up with good solutions.

Walt, on the other hand, had come ready to defend the benefits of maintaining the status quo. His folded hands rested on a pile of spreadsheets in front of him, but under the table, his foot tapped with unspent energy.

"Thanks for meeting with us, Emmett," Jack said. "How would you like to start?"

"I already know a little bit about your company, so why don't you start by telling me your concerns. If I have questions, I'll stop you." Emmett tapped a few buttons on his keyboard and looked back up at Jack, waiting for him to speak.

Jack started in on what had become a tired refrain: Sales are up, but profits are making a slow and steady decline. While he could identify some inefficiencies in purchasing and manufacturing, ultimately, he wasn't sure where they were losing money.

Adding to the problem, departments weren't communicating well with each other. Each department had their own projects that may or may not benefit other departments. They focused on what would bring success to their individual group that often had negative effects elsewhere in the company.

Sales forecasts were inaccurate and that caused ingredient shortages, which meant purchasing and production flow was disrupted and customers didn't get their product on time. Sales had to go back to their customers and changes were made, which threw off the sales forecasts and the whole thing started all over again.

Jack summed up everything by saying, "We've tried to solve the problems with more detailed spreadsheets, but so far, it hasn't seemed to help. By the time the spreadsheets are updated, there's new information. They are outdated faster than we can make them and often have errors."

"That makes sense," Emmett agreed, nodding his head thoughtfully. "Spreadsheets aren't meant to run fifty-million-dollar companies."

Walt shifted a little in his seat and Jack continued, telling Emmett of their particular sense of urgency. "My brother and sister have decided they want to claim their inheritance now and have orchestrated a takeover bid from our biggest competitor. We've bought ourselves some time, but we need to find out where the problems lie, fix them and get on with trying to save my mother's company."

"It's exactly because of this urgency," Walt added, "that we don't have the luxury of time to get people up to speed on new technology. That's why we are relying on what we're familiar with—the spreadsheets—until we can get past this buyout crisis. Then we can think about training our people to handle different kinds of tasks. When it comes down to it, I don't think our IT staff is capable of taking us through the next growth jump."

Emmett listened and occasionally took notes on his laptop.

"Deep down, I know the spreadsheets are not enough, Walt," Jack said, turning to face his CFO. "We've given them a shot and they're not working. I need information and I need it faster and more accurate than we are getting it now. If we give IT the challenge, I'm sure they would rise to it. There may be a few bumps in the road, but they'll work it out."

"You remember when we had that problem with the installation of the new EDI system and how screwed up that was," Walt countered. "We had orders getting lost or not filled, and in some cases, people weren't paid. It was a disaster. We can't afford to go through something like that again."

"Who was your project manager for that install?" Emmett interjected.

"That was Gordon, right?" Jack looked to Walt.

"Yes, our IT Manager," Walt agreed. "It was maybe a little too much for him to take on. The project took twice as long as was projected, and ended up going way over budget. And when all was said and done, there were still glitches IT couldn't solve. The software never even got used to its full potential."

Jack cringed thinking about that roll-out. It had seemed like it was more trouble than it was worth. "Gordon wasn't ready to manage that project," he admitted. "I have to take some responsibility for not recognizing that ahead of time."

"He still has a long way to go before he's ready to manage a major project," Walt said. "Right now, just handling system crashes is putting him at his limit. The IT department feels overloaded with everything it's already doing."

"You see my problem?" Jack asked turning to Emmett, who had been listening to the exchange with interest. "I feel stuck. I need better data collecting and reporting for my company to survive. I'm certain of that. But right now, I don't have the infrastructure or maybe even the budget to support making that decision." Jack threw up his arms in exasperation. "What am I supposed to do?"

Emmett shut his laptop and turned his full attention to Jack. "Your problem is not unique. In fact, I've seen it happen over and over. You're growing and successful, but at a certain point, you get stuck. You can't move forward. The amount of product you're running, the inventory that is going in and out, the numbers . . . they're too big. Any little change on one part of your production line ends up making real, and negative, impacts to sales, purchasing, and even finance and IT." Emmett looked pointedly at Walt. "It's all connected," he continued. "The spreadsheets can only take you so far, and you're past that point."

"If you are going to suggest we buy and implement a new ERP system, I need to remind you, we don't have the people in place to have a successful roll-out," Walt argued.

"Allen probably mentioned I've been working with SST Manufacturing. You've heard of them?" Jack and Walt both nodded. "Walt, their CFO had the exact same concerns as you. Their IT manager was used to dealing with downed Internet problems and the occasional small software update. Their whole department was competent enough for their current business needs, but not enough to make the growth leap SST was poised to make."

"That sounds like our IT department," Jack interjected.

"My team has been working with them for about three months now. They still have a way to go before they are able to take over and run things themselves, but with some education at the senior management level, coaching of the IT manager and contacting outside vendors to help, the changes are already quite impressive."

"How does that work?" Jack asked. "I mean, how do you get everyone on board, moving in the same direction? Right now, each of our departments kind of look after their own needs. If my Production Manager has a need, but it doesn't affect the sales department, my Sales Manager doesn't currently have an incentive to help out."

"We've set up an IT governance team and a steering committee to set priorities on projects. They've built a portfolio of projects and, together, decide what's most important. Everything is deliberate and weighed against the alternatives. This way, they can know that they're headed in the right direction and gain cooperation from every department. There's no such thing as individual or departmental projects because the steering committee helps everyone have buy-in."

"That sounds promising," Jack mused.

"I realize you've had success with SST, but how can you know the same techniques will work for Mama Meg's?" Walt wanted to know. "What if their experience is a one-off?"

"I've worked with hundreds of companies and seen similar results at each one. SST's results are the norm, not the exception," Emmett replied. "Of course there are things that make Mama Meg's unique. But the overarching principles for success are the same. When things are set up so everyone is working towards one goal, focus is put on projects that are important to the company and the right things are getting done to move the company forward."

Jack nodded, satisfied. Walt still didn't look too sure.

"This doesn't happen overnight," Emmett remarked. "But if you don't get to the root of the real challenges facing Mama Meg's, the chances that you will luck onto the right path of fixing them are slim."

"And SST Manufacturing? They're moving in the right direction now?" Walt asked, his arms folded across his chest, still unconvinced.

"They are." Emmett spoke with a contagious confidence and Jack wondered why Walt seemed immune. "They've had bumps in the road . . . don't get me wrong. I'm sure you know, Walt, that change does not happen easily."

Walt inclined his head in acknowledgement. "We've got a team of competent people running this company. We are getting a handle on how to proceed. Every process has a little trial and error. I can't justify spending money when we're probably almost at the right solution."

"So you admit, there is a problem," Emmett said, a smile in his voice. "The way I see it, you can continue to make your best guesses—the trial and error method—and maybe in six months to a year start moving towards real solutions. But then you've lost a year."

"We don't have a year to fumble around like that, Walt, and you know it," Jack declared, fighting a rise in his voice.

"Or, you can have me and someone from my team come in and have a clear and accurate picture of the state of your company in two weeks, and then start working on real solutions." Emmett looked at Jack, and then Walt, waiting for an answer, then said, "You have my card. Why don't you two talk and I can call you tomorrow."

Turning to Walt, Jack said, "You know we need this. We don't have time to figure this out on our own."

"I know. You're right," Walt admitted.

Jack turned to Emmett and asked, "How soon can we start?"

* * *

"He's going to start with a proposal," Jack explained. He'd run into Laura in the lobby as he was returning from lunch and they walked as they talked.

"And Walt was okay with this?" Laura asked, shaking her head in disbelief, keeping up with Jack's long stride.

"It's just a proposal. Walt and I will look it over, make a decision, and then share that decision with the executive team."

"Then they send people in to spy on us."

Jack thought he saw someone from HR look their direction as Laura said *spy*. "Observe. Interview. How else can they make accurate recommendations? And it will just be Emmett and one of his associates."

"How much does this service cost?"

Jack pulled out of his pocket the business card on which Emmett had written the number earlier that morning and passed it to Laura.

"Wow." Laura came to a halt in the middle of the hallway. Jack stopped and turned to face her. "And Walt's okay with this?" Laura looked at Jack for some kind of answer.

"I know it seems like a lot right now, but it will pay for itself many times over. We're losing our edge and it's only going to get worse if we don't do something now." He looked at Laura for understanding. He didn't need her approval, but he wanted it.

"I believe you. What I can't believe is that Walt is going for it. He seemed so uptight about money."

"He's the CFO. That's his job."

"I mean, he's being more tight-fisted than he normally is. Getting him to approve purchases requires an act of Congress these days."

"He's just concerned about the company and trying to find a way to turn profits back around. We can't have another losing quarter."

"And you think paying these guys to observe and interview us will help that happen?"

"I'll look at their proposal, but I'm feeling more and more convinced their feedback will be just what we need to get out of our slump."

From around the corner, someone's phone conversation became audible.

" . . . Okay. I've got to get back with Soren this afternoon anyway. I'll tell him you said so." Leslie's laughing voice drifted into the hallway and Jack realized he and Laura were standing right outside her office.

"Soren?" Laura whispered under her breath. "She's not talking about Soren Ackerman, is she?"

"How many Sorens do you know?" Jack replied, picturing the six-foot-five, 250-pound, red-cheeked, blond-haired COO of Oven Love.

"You better say something to her. If she's talking with Oven Love . . ." Laura trailed off.

"I know. It can't be good." Jack lowered his head, thinking about the implications of his Vice President of Sales talking with the COO of the competition. Was there any way this could turn out well? "Go on ahead. I'll catch up to you later." And before Laura had turned the corner, Jack was knocking on Leslie's doorframe.

"Got a minute?" he said.

"Absolutely, what do you need?" Leslie slid a clothing catalog onto what looked like Oven Love promotional material, but Jack couldn't be sure.

"I wanted to ask you about Oven Love." Jack watched for any reaction, but Leslie was as self-possessed as always. "Laura said you mentioned a few of the products they have in development last week when you went out for drinks." Jack gestured towards the chair across from Leslie's desk. "May I?" He sat down and watched as she gathered her thoughts, and then spoke.

"I needed to know what we'd be up against when we roll out our new line. As it turns out, they've already developed and tested their own line of organics and are planning on shipping to customers by the end of the month."

"How'd you find out?" Jack felt his competitive side gear up, like a revving engine. He wasn't surprised that Oven Love was going to beat them to market. It wasn't the first time, but whenever it happened, Jack swore it would be the last. He hated getting beat by that company.

"Networking. People talk." Leslie shrugged as if it were obvious.

"Are you sure? Can you trust this information?"

"Look, Jack, it's not just the product they're ahead of us on. The price they're offering... I don't know how we can match it, let alone beat it." Leslie shook her head and pushed back from her desk. She stood up and started pacing. "We don't even have a solid recipe out of R&D yet and I'm already not sure how I'm going to sell these feel-good, health-kick cookies."

Even Jack knew that price wasn't the only selling point. In the cookie business, quality and taste trumped price every time. If only there was a way to get their hands on one of Oven Love's cookies. There was no way that was going to happen, though. Oven Love would keep their new line closely guarded until it was ready to be released to the market. Mama Meg's would just have to rely on focus groups to give them feedback and hope they ended up with a superior product in enough time to grab some of the market share.

"With the huge investments we'll make in dedicated equipment and infrastructure, the higher cost of ingredients, there's no way we won't have to put a premium price on our organic line." Leslie had stopped pacing and was now facing Jack, staring and waiting as if he was supposed to answer for some great injustice. He suddenly felt like he was on the defense. "I guess I'll figure out some angle. I always do." Leslie laughed as if she had just been conspiring with him. "Of course, this would all be much easier if I had E-Sales Manager, that new CRM program, for my team. You can't expect me to work wonders with tools from last century."

How did we get on the topic of new software? Jack wondered. Then it occurred to him: Leslie was trying to distract him. He was here to find out how deep her connections to Oven Love went and what that meant for Mama Meg's, not discuss purchasing a half-million-dollar sales software package. He was done beating around the bush.

"What's going on with you and Oven Love, Leslie? You've got your hands on confidential information only a handful of people inside the company even know about. You're not getting this stuff from networking." Jack asked, trying to pull the conversation back to the essential topic. "And now you're talking to Soren, aren't you?" Leslie at least had the good grace to look abashed.

"I've been in contact with Soren, but it's not what you think," she stated, sinking back into her chair. "We went to university together. There's some history between us." She looked at Jack with raised brows that seemed to fill in the rest of the story, but Jack wanted her to say it anyway.

"Explain," he said, folding his arms across his chest.

"We dated . . . for about three years." Something like regret tinged her voice. "After graduation, we both got jobs and were advancing. The problem was, we were both very competitive—not just in our careers, but our relationship, too. It was a great way to grow a career, but a total relationship killer. I'm surprised we stayed together as long as we did."

"And now?" Jack asked, impatient to get past the soap opera and to some answers.

"We're friends," she replied, and then added, "Really. That's all it is," when Jack's narrowed eyes told her he wasn't sold.

"The kind of friends who share corporate secrets?"

"Jack, come on. You know me better than that. I would never betray Mama Meg's." She actually sounded hurt at the accusation.

"Yet Soren's shared confidential Oven Love information with you? Am I supposed to think he's not getting anything in return?"

Leslie, for once, had no response.

"I'm looking at the biggest fight of my career. If I can't turn things around in a year, I'm going to lose this company. I can't afford to have people on my team who aren't behind me, one hundred percent, Leslie." Jack shook his head, astonished at finding himself in this conversation, and stared at the ceiling for a moment, gathering his thoughts.

After a few seconds he spoke, "I have to know, Leslie. Are you with me?"

She didn't answer right away, but when she did, her conviction was clear. "I know people see me as a bit of a rebel, but I didn't get to where I am now by always playing by the rules. You don't gain an edge on the competition without a little," she cleared her throat and said, "creativity."

Jack didn't know where she was going with this. What was she trying to say?

"You can count on this, Jack," she continued. "I'm always going to think creatively to gain an edge, and I'm with you. One hundred percent."

5

Getting to the Point

"I want you to meet Emmett Trask," Jack said to his team sitting around the conference room table. They all appeared to be sizing up Emmett in their own way. Leslie was casually scrolling on her phone, undoubtedly Googling him, while Marcia appeared impressed with his crisply ironed shirt and neatly stacked brochures. Laura and Chris each glanced at each other, whispered—Jack could only guess what—and laughed quietly to themselves. Walt leaned back in his chair, arms folded, as if still waiting to be convinced, while Gordon, the IT Manager, glanced nervously at Emmett, then at his hands folded in his lap, and back again. His knee bounced with an anxious rhythm.

"As you know, Emmett is going to help us identify where some of the breakdowns are that are creating so many struggles as we try and grow this company. As part of that, he's going to take some time to meet with each of you and talk about what challenges you face, what is working for you and where you think we might be able to improve." Jack turned to Emmett. "Do you have anything to add?"

Emmett faced all who were gathered around the table. "I appreciate the opportunity to try and help Mama Meg's. This may seem like an intrusion of your time, but I just want to assure you that your feedback will be the most valuable tool in helping me evaluate your processes and make suggestions for improvement." His smile was warm and reassuring. "My goal is to come up with a strategy to help this company get over the hurdles to growth that are currently in front of you. Of course the ball is still very much in your court. Any suggestions I make will need to meet with your approval. It's completely up to you how you implement them."

Out of the corner of his eye, Jack could have sworn he saw Walt roll his eyes.

* * *

"You know what my issues are," Jack said to Emmett, who sat across the table from him. "I've got to make more money, but I don't know what to sell to do it. Do I put our energy into creating new product when we're struggling to keep up with what we're already making?"

Emmett nodded with understanding.

"It's like I pointed out during our walk-through. Chris's guys are using the home-brewed MRP-like system to manage their manufacturing workflow needs, but the information that goes in and comes out of that system is only used for their department. It's not driving the SCADA system."

"Remind me what that does, again," Emmett asked, taking out a pen and scribbling something on his notepad.

"Essentially, the SCADA runs all our machines remotely. Every time Chris sets up the line for a different cookie, new parameters have to be entered into the SCADA by hand. If there are breakdowns someone has to go out and read hundreds of dials and diagnose and try to fix the problem. Do you know how much room there is for error when we do things that way?" Jack rubbed the back of his neck as if to ease the pain this problem had become, then continued, "And neither of those software tools are connected to our ERP system. I feel like I'm making decisions blind. I need more data, but . . ." He threw up his hands, ". . . I don't know where to start."

"If all goes well, that's what I hope to figure out this week," Emmett responded. "It's possible you're too close to the situation to see clearly. I'll find out more, though, as I do my evaluation." He closed his laptop and pushed back his chair. "After I have a chance to talk to everyone on your executive team, I should be able to give you a clear picture of where your breakdowns are and what needs to be fixed."

"Who do you see first?"

Emmett swiped at his phone a couple times and then answered, "I'm meeting with Leslie in five minutes."

"You'll let me know how it goes at the end of the day?" Jack asked.

Emmett nodded. "Don't worry. I've worked with lots of different companies, each with their own set of issues. I'm sure that, together, we'll figure things out."

Jack felt a little of the tension relax out of his shoulders. If Emmett really could figure out the problem, Jack could turn things around and there still might be time enough to save the company. "I'll see you this afternoon, then." Jack shook Emmett's hand and walked him to the door. "And good luck with Leslie," Jack said.

Emmett smiled—a little naively, Jack thought—and made his way down the hall towards Leslie's office.

You'll need it, Jack thought, wondering if Emmett would be a match for her fast talking.

* * *

"Why don't you start off by telling me a little bit about what you do here at Mama Meg's," Emmett inquired.

"I'm the Vice President of Sales. I oversee nineteen sales people and it's my job to get customers and make this company money." Leslie shifted, settling into her chair across the desk from Emmett and continued. "Right now I'm considering the feasibility of territory expansion..."

"You want to sell Mama Meg's cookies in more states than you currently are?" he asked. "I don't mean to interrupt. I just wanted to make sure I understand. Mama Meg's is a regional product right now, correct?" Emmett's gaze drifted across the numerous sales award plaques lining Leslie's walls.

"Right. I've been working with Marcia, our marketing VP, pretty closely to see if we're ready for a national campaign."

Emmett uncrossed his legs, then re-crossed them on the other side, repositioning himself in his chair. "Tell me about the challenges you're facing. What would you say your biggest business problem is?"

"That's easy. I don't have a CRM system," she declared, folding her arms and leaning back. "I don't know what's in inventory so I don't know what my guys can sell. I literally have to check with Chris before I can accept an order. This holds up my whole process and delays my close. If we just had some sales software, Chris would have an idea of what our sales projections are and he wouldn't have to make small batches of product based on past sales, but could actually make the right amount of product based on actual sales and projections.

"I can't continue this way. Chris and I are in a position where we are constantly at each other's throats. He's upset with me for not communicating our sales projections better, and I'm livid when he doesn't have the product to fulfill our orders. If Jack wants this business to keep growing, I've got to have a CRM system. Period."

"A CRM system seems to make sense." Leslie smiled and relaxed a little, looking smug at having just gained an ally. But Emmett continued, "Let me ask you this: Is your sales process documented?"

A little of the previous confidence drained from her face. "Of course it is. I mean, we've got most of it documented. Well . . . some of it. Why do you ask?"

"If your company decides to hire my consulting firm for the next step, we'll want to take a look at your current documented processes to understand how implementing a CRM system will impact them. We'll need to make sure that your current processes are built into the system."

"Of course. That makes sense." Leslie scribbled a quick note on a sticky note on her desk. "So, have you done any of these kinds of system implementations before? Do you have ideas of what kinds of software is best?"

Emmett looked up from taking notes on his laptop and said, "I worked with many companies that had an integrated sales management and MRP system, and the info flowed pretty well between the two; is that what you're looking for?"

"If it helps Sales and Production cooperate and communicate, I'm all for it," Leslie agreed, leaning forward a little in her chair, her voice lowering to a conspiratorial level. "I just need to get everyone else to see how important it is."

* * *

"I've got to take this," Jack said, and excused himself from a meeting as soon as he saw John Linde's name on his caller ID.

Jack answered and without ceremony John spoke, "We have a situation."

All the potential disasters ran through Jack's head at breakneck speed. Had there been a food recall from one of their suppliers? The fallout could be devastating. Or maybe it was from one of their competitors? Was Oven Love infringing on one of their copyrights? The last thing he needed now was more headaches from Oven Love. "What's up?" Jack asked, bracing for the worst.

"It's Scott," John replied.

Is he trying to renege on the deal? Jack wondered how much bigger of a pain his brother was capable of being.

"He's been in an accident."

* * *

"So, how are things in the Marketing department?" Emmett asked Marcia across her tidy desk. "I understand from Leslie that you're looking at expanding to other states?"

She reached behind her to a file cabinet, opened a drawer, and almost without looking pulled out a neatly labeled folder and opened it. "This is an ad we ran in Sunset Magazine *for three months in the Pacific Northwest Region. It cost us $233,400. I have no way of knowing our return on that ad. Did it increase revenue? There is no way to track and report that."*

Marcia reached into her drawer again and pulled out another folder and opened it. "Here's a campaign we ran in the Seattle market." Marcia spread out a series of grocery store fliers, coupons and mailers so Emmett could see. "Did it work? I have no clue. The grocery chain loved working with us and said they got a good response, but 'a good response' is not enough for me to use in my planning process. It's not enough to know if the brand is growing or can support a price increase."

Emmett thought for a minute. "Have you thought about using one of those national databases that collect grocery store data? I understand there are several that are well-respected in the industry and have great information on sales and pricing." He punched the keys on his keyboard, waited and then, turning his laptop so Marcia could see the webpage he'd pulled up and said, "Something like this?"

Marcia perked up as she looked at the screen. "I've been thinking about this exact thing and have asked Gordon to look into it," she answered. "That would help with general information, but I really need a way to use our own data and, right now, I just don't have a way to capture that."

Emmett watched as she carefully reorganized the folders, closed them up and returned them to their spot in the file cabinet. "It sounds like you're saying there needs to be a better way to track and report data so it can be used to improve and plan marketing campaigns."

"Exactly."

* * *

"What do you mean 'an accident'?" Jack asked. "In his car?"

"Yes, it happened early this morning. Three a.m., out on Marine Drive."

"What was he doing driving around at three a.m. on a Wednesday morning?"

"It appears he was trying to work off a night of drinking."

"He was drunk? Did he hurt anyone? Is he okay?"

"He's got some cuts and bruises, but is otherwise okay. His car is totaled . . ." John let that last part hang, as if unfinished.

"So no one else was involved? He didn't hit another driver?" Could there be a ray of sunlight in this terrible, black cloud?

"No one else was involved in the accident," John stated. "He ran into a fire hydrant. Water everywhere. Fire department came, and then the police showed up as well. He was arrested, of course. Booked on DUI and aggravated assault."

"Wait, what? Aggravated assault. I thought you said no one else was involved."

John paused, then spoke "He threw a punch at the arresting officer."

* * *

"Chris, Laura," Emmett said, extending his hand to each, "I know you're both very busy. Thank you so much for your time." He took a chair in Chris's office, while the rhythmic thrum of packing machines provided a dull chant through the closed door. Chris was at his desk and Laura in a chair to his left. "Why don't you start by explaining what you see as your challenges."

"Let me put it to you this way," Chris started. "If I don't get enough information from Sales, I can't manage my supply chain. They have no idea when or how much they're going to sell and so it's impossible for me to have what they need, when they need it." He exhaled sharply and ran his hand through his hair. "It's a vicious circle."

"In the past, I've been able to rely on data from past years to predict how much product to make," added Laura. "But not now. When the sales forecast is off, we can't order raw materials accurately, it's too late to get good prices on our raw materials—the ingredients we use to make all our cookies. I can't just call up and order tons of flour and expect to get it in a few days. Those orders are placed months in advance, while the wheat is still in the ground on some farm in Idaho. Ideally, I place my order for the year and that's it. It's the most cost effective way to buy. But when we don't get the right sales data, our purchasing is off and we run out of flour with four months left in our year." She shook her head and shrugged.

"Tell me more about that," Emmett queried while tapping out notes on his laptop.

Chris spoke up. "When we don't have ingredients, we have to stop production. Sometimes we have a total work stoppage—I have to send guys home until we get what we need. Other times, though, we can start production on another cookie."

"That sounds good," Emmett said.

"Actually, it's worse for efficiency," Laura replied, shaking her head. "We have to break down the old line, manually type in the recipe and set up for the new product. It takes hours, if not days, to get it all done. Then as soon as the ingredients come in for the product we were supposed to be working on, we've got to break down and set up all over again."

"I feel like I'm having to do my job with one hand tied behind my back," Chris sighed, shoulders slumped.

* * *

"He what?" Jack exclaimed, wondering if his brain would catch up with his ears.

"Mind you, it wasn't a good punch. Barely even made contact. I did mention he'd been drinking for a while." John's sigh seemed to say he was getting too old for this. "But it was enough for the assault charge," he finally finished.

"Where is he now?"

"He's in the county jail. I've got someone down there now working on bail. He should be out in a few hours."

Jack was incredulous. *This* was the guy who was poised to take down his company? An irresponsible idiot who couldn't even manage his own life without screwing it up. How was this happening? "Well," he finally said. "No rush."

* * *

"So, Walt," Emmett asked, "tell me about your role at Mama Meg's. I'm guessing, as the person here with the longest tenure, you've seen a lot."

"I've been with Mama Meg's from the beginning. I helped Meg get this company off the ground." Walt let out a short laugh that didn't seem to reach his eyes. "Back then, Jack would come in after school and help on the production floor, sweeping, running errands between departments. Now he's the CEO." It seemed like Walt wanted to say more, but he adjusted himself in his chair and went on. "It's easy to point your finger and say where you want a ship to go, but it's a whole other thing to make sure the ship has the money to get there."

"And that's how you see your role here at the company?" Emmett seemed to wonder if there was something more to what Walt was saying.

"I'm just a numbers guy." Walt's chuckle was genuine. "It's what I'm good at. Like I said, I've been doing it for Mama Meg's for years and I know this company like I know my own child—I've been here through the lean years, seen the growth and, personally, I'm proud of what it's become."

"And how would you say things are going now?"

"Listen," he leaned forward, resting his elbows on his knees, hands clasped. "Keeping things in the black is never easy. Of course there are challenges, especially with a company this size." Walt paused, considering his next words carefully. "You know I'm not in favor of this . . . consultation . . ." Walt accented the word with air quotes. "I think the bumps in the road we are experiencing now are just growing pains that we will work through on our own. A new ERP system isn't going to fix things. Every time we've tried to implement new software it's been a disaster." He ticked off his reasons on his fingers. "Getting everyone up to speed often takes a full year. Routines are disrupted and mistakes crop up while we deal with the learning curve. And these systems are expensive. I don't think the loss of productivity is worth the minimal time saving or data collection benefits an ERP system would provide."

Emmett took his time before responding. "I appreciate your cooperation despite your reservations, Walt. I'm not sure what the right solution for Mama Meg's is at this time. Maybe a new ERP system will be the answer, or maybe I will have other recommendations to make. But the only way I can know for sure the best thing for Mama Meg's is to get honest feedback, like yours, from everyone I speak with."

Walt bowed his head in acquiescence that appeared to come from validation.

"Do you have any specific examples of challenges to your department . . . because of Mama Meg's growth? How have you been able to keep up?" Emmett asked.

"I have staffing issues. We bring in these young Millennials and they're not used to how a company this size doesn't respond at the speed of a smartphone app. Things take a little longer." Walt sat back in his chair and folded his arms. "They're not getting our monthly numbers into the system in a timely manner. Sometimes I can't close the books for three weeks after the end of the month."

"And this is because your staff isn't efficient?"

"Exactly," Walt answered, somewhat satisfied, but then added, "Of course they'd say it was our software that was inefficient. But it's served us fine for years and never been a problem."

"And that's your only challenge?"

"Pretty much."

"What about the bank? Do you feel like you have the information they need? For your reports?" Emmett saved his notes and started to close his laptop, then stopped when Walt spoke.

"I have always had to make estimates and judgment calls when dealing with the bank. That's nothing new. Sure, it's a little more difficult now when they want to know where we are with our line of credit, for example. More information would be helpful in that regard. But this is what they pay me for. I have the experience and the knowledge to make those kinds of judgment calls even when all the information isn't there."

* * *

"We have a bigger problem on our hands, Jack," John said. "The news media thinks your brother would make a good story. There are reporters there now, at the county jail, just waiting for the moment he walks out the door to try and get him to say something."

"Scott McCallister may be a first-class pain in the ass, but he is not news."

"They disagree." John cleared his throat. Jack could hear papers shuffling on the other end. "'Scott McCallister, son of late Margaret McCallister, founder of Mama Meg's Cookies and hailed by many as the Cookie Queen of the Northwest, was arrested for DUI and aggravated assault early Wednesday morning' . . ."

"Are you reading the newspaper?" Jack asked, feeling more and more like this phone conversation had to be nothing more than a stress-induced nightmare.

"It's buried on the back page. Barely two paragraphs long. But I guess it's a slow news day because all three local stations have picked up on the story and are now waiting for your brother to get out of jail. This is five o'clock news material, Jack."

* * *

"Gordon, good to meet you," Emmett said, extending his hand to the IT Manager. "I'm eager to hear how things are going in the IT department."

"Busy," Gordon replied. "Always busy."

"Tell me more about what keeps you so busy."

"Everybody wants something," Gordon started. "I've got a major project from the Marketing department. Marcia has been wanting me to find a national database of grocery store sales and customer information. Then there's Sales: Leslie always wants her sales people to have the latest and greatest everything. Phones, tablets, laptops," he ticked the items off on his fingers. "And every time there is a software update or phone upgrade, it takes days to get it taken care of. We're spending at least half to three-quarters of our time maintaining PCs, servers, laptops and the network that ties them all together. I just don't have enough resources to keep the infrastructure running and work on installing and maintaining the applications that people need to do their jobs more efficiently."

Emmett nodded and continued to listen.

"Chris has projects he wants me working on and he thinks his are more important than Leslie's or Marcia's. It's not uncommon to have guys in my department working ten-, twelve-hour days, regularly."

"Do you think it's a staffing issue? Do you need more people?"

"Sometimes I feel like we could never have enough people in this department to handle everything. It seems like something needs to happen at a different level. Maybe in the way jobs get requested. I'm just getting it from all sides, all at the same time."

"Well, this is certainly good information for me to have. Have you come up with any ideas for ways to improve the situation?"

"I barely have time to stop and think. Most of the time I'm concerned about turnover if things stay as busy as they've been. For the most part, the people on my team are busting their butts every day. I don't know how long they can maintain the pace before burning out." Gordon looked off into the distance at nothing in particular, then shook his head and looked back at Emmett with tired eyes.

"Well," Emmett started, "I can help you right now with the national grocery store database. One of my clients is using—and happy with—this company here." Emmett slid a scrap of paper with a name written on it across the table. "Give them a quick look. I think they'll be a good fit for Marcia."

Gordon read the slip of paper and nodded. "Thanks. This will help."

"You said your team is working hard 'for the most part,'" Emmett continued. "What did you mean by that? Do you have some who aren't pulling their weight?"

"Oh, you know. There are always a few who need a little more direction, but . . ." He stopped, as if unwilling to continue.

"But what?" Emmett asked.

Gordon shook his head as if he was unsure about going on. "It's Scott McCallister. I know you're going to be reporting to Jack everything we all say, and I didn't want to bring it up... but his brother... I'm sorry, but I would have fired him long ago if I could have. It's not just that he does a bad job. His attitude is like a disease that has spread. He's the boss's brother. Everyone knows that. When they see him acting irresponsibly, coming in late, leaving early, doing a half-assed job at best on any task he's given, it's bad for morale."

"Hmm." Emmett rubbed his chin, typed and said, "That doesn't make your job easy."

"No, it doesn't. At least he takes a lot of 'sick' days," Gordon responded, making quotes with his fingers. "When he's gone, it's just one less thing for me to have to deal with."

"Is he here today?" Emmett asked.

"Nope. Hasn't called in, hasn't showed up. I have no idea where he is and I don't really care."

* * *

"Is there any way he can go out a back door to avoid the media?" Jack asked.

"My guy down there working on bail says they've got all the doors covered and there is not going to be a way to avoid them."

"Mama Meg's doesn't need this right now. I don't need this negative publicity. They're going to say he's an employee of the company, aren't they?"

"I don't know what they plan to say, Jack."

"I don't think Scott should be opening his mouth in front of a camera right now. Or ever. Who knows what might come out."

"My guy will go over all that with him. There will be a car waiting. We'll take care of this," he said with warmth and conviction that Jack found calming. That's what John had done for years, after all, was take care of his mom and this company. He would do it again.

"Thanks, John," he said gratefully. "Thanks for handling this." He knew it was ridiculous, but sometimes he felt his mother's presence when he talked with John, as if she was still taking care of her company through him. This was one of those times.

"Of course, Jack. You know you and your family are much more to me than clients. I'll always do what I can for you." Jack thought he could hear a smile creak out across John's aged face and the thought made him grin. Then John added, "But you're going to want to hire a PR agency."

* * *

"How did the interviews go?" Jack asked, ushering Emmett into his office.

"Very well. How about your day?" Emmett sat down and flipped open his computer.

"I've definitely had better." Jack sat at his desk and drummed his fingers for a few beats before asking, "So what did you learn?"

Emmett summed up his meetings with Leslie, Marcia, Chris, Laura, Walt and Gordon while Jack listened, barely registering any emotion. There were no surprises.

"I'll have my recommendations ready to present to your team in a couple weeks, but what I'm looking for is that gap between where you are now, and where you need to be. Then I can give you a road map for how to eliminate it."

Jack nodded, but wasn't sure he understood. "So where are we supposed to be? How big is this gap?"

"Right now, Walt is determining what Gordon's priorities should be, but Walt has a limited view of what is right for the company as a whole. IT can't be as productive because it's spinning its wheels on projects that are important to individuals, but not important to the whole."

"So how do we fix that?"

"My first thoughts are that you need a Chief Information Officer along with an IT Governance process. You don't have an IT leader who understands business and can communicate well with all department heads. And, you don't have a system in place to assess the priority of different projects—there is no map for what is most important and how it's going to get done. An IT Governance team would help with that."

Jack exhaled and nodded.

"You also need a more responsive ERP system, one that will be able to work for everyone—not just your finance department—and take Mama Meg's where it needs to go."

"Okay." Jack's fingers drummed the table. He was getting answers and it felt good. He felt like he could finally get some traction and stop spinning his wheels, working hard to move Mama Meg's forward, but getting nowhere.

"There's another thing," Emmett said, looking Jack in the eye. "Gordon, your IT Manager. He's a good guy, and working hard— probably a little too hard—but he doesn't have the experience to run an organization like yours that is poised to double in size. He needs help and mentoring. That's one of the things a CIO would help with."

"Alright. That makes sense."

"Well, there's one more thing," Emmett stated, pausing.

"What is it?"

"Gordon mentioned he spends more time than he should on one employee who isn't pulling their weight. It's causing a serious morale problem in that department."

Jack sighed heavily and shook his head in resignation. "It's Scott, isn't it?"

"That's what I've heard."

There was a long moment of silence as Jack mentally added one more offense to Scott's running list.

"I'll need to look at my notes and give it some more thought," Emmett said. "I should have my full recommendations to you in a couple of weeks. But off the record, something needs to be done with your brother."

6

The Honing Process

"I'm going to fire Scott," Jack declared, walking into Laura's office. He didn't bother to sit down. He needed to stand up for this.

"Because of his DUI? Jack, I know he's a little reckless in his personal life, but he shouldn't get fired for *that*," Laura countered, shuffling a few papers around on her desk. "Besides, I think he's learned his lesson. You let him sit in jail for a whole day!"

"If it had been up to me, I would have left him in there longer! He could have killed someone, Laura." Jack took a deep breath to calm himself and continued, "But that's not why I'm firing him. He's been a drain on the IT department for a while now. I've suspected as much, but hoped it would work itself out. As if Scott would ever work to better himself when he thought a handout was available."

"How bad is it? Maybe we can talk to him. Let him know he needs to do better."

"We're beyond that. It's been nearly a year of unacceptable behavior. Any other employee would have been terminated months ago."

Jack could almost see the gears working in Laura's head, and then the click. "But it's *Scott McCallister*," she exclaimed, leaning back in her chair. "They can't fire the CEO's brother."

"Exactly. Scott McCallister." Jack didn't even make an effort to keep the disdain from his voice. Over the last few weeks, Scott had been on the evening news, the subject of a two-hour radio talk show, and even trended on Twitter with the hashtag "#badcookie." Jack had spent hours on the phone with John discussing the details of Scott's bail, court hearing and possible legal outcomes. Even Gordon—although reluctant at first—had filled him in on how Scott was sabotaging the IT department with more than enough offenses to justify termination. Thoughts of his self-absorbed, mess of a brother even stole many of the hours Jack should have been sleeping. He was sick and tired of Scott.

"Maybe we can place him somewhere else?" Laura offered. She pulled her laptop over and clicked open the org chart, as if Scott's next opportunity would suddenly materialize.

"You think he'd do well in Production? You think Chris might be able to turn him around?"

"No!" she declared quickly, then, recovering a bit, added, "Not Production." Laura thought a minute. "What about Sales? He couldn't mess that up, could he? Maybe working on commission would be an incentive for him? It could be the thing that will finally motivate him to grow up and take some responsibility."

"Laura, I'm not putting someone who wants to sell our company to Oven Love in the Sales department." Jack tried to put himself in Laura's shoes. He knew she had a soft spot in her heart for her family. But he also knew she was good at her job. Damn good. She wouldn't allow that soft spot to get in the way of business.

"Scott is part of the reason Mama Meg's is having such a hard time right now." At this obvious oversimplification Laura shot Jack a sideways glance dripping with skepticism. "Granted, he's a small part, but there is no doubt that he is dragging down IT, and if we are going to work through this slump, we need IT to be strong."

Laura looked down at her hands, folded in her lap, and said nothing. Finally she sighed. "When?"

"Tonight. He has a meeting with John before his hearing tomorrow. I'll have payroll cut his last paycheck, pick him up from John's and take him home. I'll tell him then."

"Oh, Jack." There was pleading in Laura's voice. "That sounds so harsh. Can't you wait until after the hearing?"

"Is there ever a good time to get fired by your brother?" Jack finally sat down, lowering himself with an air of defeat into the chair across from her desk.

Laura covered her face in her hands, then pulled them away and said, "You're right. Dammit, you're right." She looked up at the ceiling, collecting herself, then back at Jack. "I hate this."

"I know you do."

* * *

Jack walked into Emmett's presentation with Laura, their conversation about Scott having morphed into a discussion about Brigitte's irresponsible spending habits before coming around to the recommendations Emmett had sent over a few days earlier. Jack had had time to look them over and ask questions, so he knew what to expect.

Emmett was already there, setting up. "Good afternoon," he said. "You ready for this?"

"Absolutely. I'm sure everyone is going to see the wisdom behind your recommendations. They just make sense," Jack replied.

"Well, that sounds intriguing," Leslie said as she entered the conference room, the smile on her face not quite reaching her eyes. "Did you recommend a CRM system for Sales?" She looked at Emmett, waiting for an answer she already knew.

"Have a seat, Leslie," Jack offered. "We'll be getting started soon enough."

Chris and Marcia arrived moments later and Jack turned the floor over to Emmett.

"I've learned a lot from talking with each of you and your teams a couple of weeks back," Emmett started. "Because of the information you provided, I have a good picture of what is keeping Mama Meg's from bridging the gap between the 50-million-dollar-a-year company you are right now, and the 100-million-dollar-a-year company you want to grow to at the next level."

Emmett passed out reports to each person at the table. Jack watched as everyone turned to the first page and started looking things over.

"As you can see in this summary, my recommendations are for Mama Meg's to form a strong IT Governance Committee. You may have been able to slide by without one up to this point, but going forward, if this company is to grow successfully through the right IT investments, you need to have a committee that will look at the needs of individual departments, then consider and prioritize them for the good of the whole company."

There was some murmuring from Walt's side of the room, but Emmett pressed forward. "Second, your ERP system needs to be updated or replaced. I haven't spent enough time to know which, but I can help you find out. It may be that we can add a few modules to get it working for everyone, which would save money and time." Jack could practically see everyone's minds filling with questions and rebuttals, but Emmett wasn't done yet.

Surprisingly, Walt nodded as if he were finally hearing something that made sense. Jack chuckled under his breath. Was that old grump finally coming around?

"You need to outsource management of your IT infrastructure - networks and computers. Gordon needs to refocus. His department is stretched too thin and, ultimately, their time will be better spent implementing the new ERP modules, not fixing computers, updating software and acting as tech support," continued Emmett. "Any of these recommendations on their own would be a tremendous amount of work for your team to manage and execute, yet they are crucial if Mama Meg's is going to continue to scale and grow. That's why my final suggestion is to bring in a Chief Information Officer—someone who can lead and guide the IT department."

Emmett stopped for a beat, and then carried on, "My report has detailed information on each of these recommendations, but why don't you let me know what you're thinking so far. Are there any questions? Thoughts?"

"I'll be honest with you, Emmett. I wasn't too thrilled with the idea of paying for a consultant to come in and tell us to spend even more money," Walt declared.

"You could have fooled me," Chris chuckled. Marcia laughed and Laura patted Walt on the back good-naturedly.

"Look," he said, trying to be serious, "I'm the one that looks out for the money. I know it doesn't make me the most popular guy at the table, but someone's got to do it."

"And you're very good at what you do, Walt," Jack said, his tone reassuring, but still amused. "Could it be that you've seen the wisdom in bringing in Emmett?"

"I love the idea of updating our existing ERP system," Walt said. "This isn't something I had considered. I had assumed it was either spend hundreds of thousands of dollars and a year or more on a new ERP implementation, or stick with the underperforming, ineffectual system we have now."

"So, you admit it is not effective?" Jack asked, enjoying very much this "Come to Jesus" moment Walt was having.

"I never said the ERP system worked well. I just said I didn't want to replace it. Emmett's come up with an option I had never considered." Walt sat back in his chair, his arms folded across his chest and a stony look on his face.

For a moment, everyone sat, staring at Walt, unsure of what to say about his change in thinking. Then Walt's granite grimace began to crack and a smile slowly grew across his face.

"That still needs to be determined," Emmett reminded him. "But I think there's a possibility that will be the case."

"If we do update," Walt inquired, "what is the time frame for getting everyone up to speed?"

"It might only take six months, as opposed to a year or more if you started from scratch with a new system."

There was a palpable shift in the collective mood of the whole room.

"There's a module I heard about that will help me track marketing metrics. Would I be able to get that?" Marcia asked.

"What about a CRM module?" Leslie interjected. "Sales *has* to have a CRM module."

"And I could use a better MRP system. Would they have something like that available? We desperately need better reporting," Chris said.

"What I can do is document your requirements, take a look at your current system and compare it with other systems on the market. But what we are eventually looking at is a system that will provide you with a dashboard so you know at a glance all the information that is relevant to your department. There will be mobile apps . . ."

"I like the sound of this already," Leslie agreed. "That is, as long as I get my module for Sales."

"We will build a *needs* list—not a wish list." Emmett looked around the room to make sure everyone understood. "You'll actually have to support why you need the module, software, or whatever it is you want. But once we get that list, the IT Governance Committee can decide and prioritize based on what's best for the company as a whole. That's why governance is so important. Each individual department needs to move forward, not only with what is best for them individually, but also for the good of Mama Meg's. Without oversight, it's nearly impossible to reach that goal."

Out of the corner of his eye, Jack saw Leslie roll her eyes and look at Marcia. Fortunately, Emmett caught it, too. "I know what you're thinking, Leslie," he said as Leslie sat up a little straighter in her chair, quickly composing herself. "You don't have time for another meeting."

"Well, it's true. My time is so tied up in meetings already and most of them, frankly, are a waste of time." Leslie glanced at Jack and said, "No offense, Jack."

"Right now, the decisions you are making are sub-optimized. IT only has time to listen to the squeaky wheel, and that's who ends up getting the grease. That's not necessarily the way it should go. *Governance removes IT from the decision-making so the right projects get done.*"

Jack spoke up. "We've been throwing money at so many different things, but not really knowing for sure if they are the best way to move us forward as a company. The IT department has had to be reactionary—so tied up with just trying to get to the bottom of their to-do list that they haven't been able to spend time working on the things that really matter. That has to stop."

"Exactly," Emmett agreed. "Let me put it to you this way: Imagine you've just bought a Lamborghini to drive to work every day but your commute is bumper-to-bumper traffic. That beautiful engine never reaches anything higher than twenty miles per hour, the tires never get to grip the road through a sharp curve and you will never know the superior handling and ride from the advanced suspension. If that's all you ever do with your Lamborghini, you've just thrown $300,000 down the toilet."

Chris was nodding as Emmett continued. He got it.

"Without the right direction," Emmett explained, "IT is a Lamborghini that never goes over twenty miles per hour. Yes, my recommendations include spending money. But governance will allow you to know for sure you're getting the most bang for your buck."

"So far, I like what I'm hearing," Walt said, swiveling in his chair to face Emmett. "The Governance Committee is long overdue and I love the idea that our current ERP might be able to serve us with some upgrades. But I don't understand the need for a CIO. To me it sounds like another salary to pay out for something I'm currently doing."

"I'm actually suggesting a part-time, temporary CIO, Walt," Emmett said. "Think of it as a one-time investment, not another salary."

"Yes, but what can a CIO do that I'm not already doing?" Walt tapped his fingers on the arm of his chair.

"This person would act as a consultant and mentor. His role would be to make recommendations on how to work towards your shared goals, to lead and establish a pace. He would also act as a mentor to Gordon."

"What does Gordon need a mentor for?" Leslie asked. "He seems to be doing just fine in his role."

"You will need a full-time CIO eventually and Gordon may be able to step into that role. But right now he has a long way to go before he's ready." He clicked over to the next slide that showed a list of qualities needed in a CIO. "You need someone that is going to add true business value to Mama Meg's, not just manage the IT department. A CIO needs to have a very strong planning focus to leverage the constantly changing technology landscape. He or she will need to have excellent communication skills and be comfortable working and building relationships with other executives. He or she should have strong leadership and people development skills." Emmett continued reading down the list. "They must think strategically and focus on business transformation through technology to take it to the next level. And of course, the right CIO will have a solid technical background and knowledge of IT processes."

Emmett turned back to Walt and continued. "For now, Walt, Gordon will continue to report to you. The interim CIO would not have signature authority and he can't fire anyone."

Too bad, Jack thought, imagining how nice it would be to delegate Scott's termination to someone else.

". . . he will be able to hit the ground running," Emmett continued, "since he specializes in helping companies just like yours through struggles with growth. And he only stays until your business goals have been reached. Then he's done."

"To tell you the truth," Walt said, "I don't know what those IT guys are asking when they come to me most of the time. If you're not working with the technology day in and day out, it's hard to keep up. I guess bringing in someone who understands this stuff better makes sense."

Laura spoke up. "I'm not sure I see the wisdom in outsourcing some of our IT. It seems like a big expense when we already have people in-house to handle things that come up. Isn't that why we have an IT department in the first place?"

"Because IT has had to focus on things like software upgrades and solving computer problems, they haven't had any time to focus on higher value projects like new products, business process reengineering and revenue generating projects," Emmett said. "Let's go back to our Lamborghini. You buy a

Lamborghini because of what it can do for you: speed, handling, suspension. You don't use it to sit in traffic. When IT spends all its time updating software, they are a Lamborghini sitting in traffic. It makes sense to outsource your operational processes so your team can focus on their core competencies."

"We're already outsourcing payroll, and that's been a huge money-saver for us," Walt pointed out.

"Good point," Marcia agreed. "I'd almost forgotten about that."

"That's because it's seamless," Walt said. "Payroll is important, but does nothing to grow the business. It's busywork. Why not let someone else handle that?"

"Exactly, Walt," Emmett said. "Outsourcing IT to outside experts would get rid of the busywork and allow Gordon and his team to focus on the things that really help Mama Meg's to grow."

"So, if they don't handle all the basic stuff, what are some of the things they'll be doing?" Laura asked. Jack sensed she was beginning to see the insight in Emmett's ideas, but just needed a little more convincing.

"IT will administer the ERP modules. They can add enhancements and upgrades as needed. They will work with departments in training scenarios on how to use those modules more effectively. Once the day-to-day duties have been outsourced, many IT people will act more as business analysts, interfacing between technology and the business side of things. Their role becomes helping everyone get the most out of the systems and software. They can explain how to generate reports and how to collect the right kind of data."

"How would an IT outsourcing company work, then?" Walt asked. "What types of things would they handle?"

"Contractors will install monitoring software on the servers so they can remotely monitor your systems. Some of the contractors may be on-site, but for the most part, they will be off-site, handling the desktops and networks and providing basic help desk. Ideally, once we've got the ERP where we want it, it will be moved to a private cloud so everything is handled remotely, in real time."

"This is sounding better and better," Laura said.

"Yes," Marcia agreed. "I'm starting to wonder why we didn't have you help us earlier, Emmett."

"That's not all," Emmett said. "Ideally, each of you would have a customized dashboard on your computer that tells you exactly what is going on in real time. Leslie, yours would be specific to the Sales department, while Jack's might have more of a broad overview. Everyone would get the information most relevant to their needs."

If the atmosphere in the room had been steadily warming to Emmett's ideas, now it burst into a flame of enthusiasm. Chris and Laura immediately started discussing the possibilities for Production, while Leslie and Marcia were excitedly chatting, making lists of data they wanted access to on their dashboards.

Walt was actually smiling. "How soon can we start?" he asked.

"The first thing we should do is create a Governance Committee," Jack said. "I'll be contacting those of you I think should participate. From there we can look at how to implement the different recommendations."

"I've got the names of several part-time CIOs you can consider. And of course I'll work with whomever you choose to help evaluate your current ERP system," Emmett offered.

Jack couldn't wait to talk to Allen and let him know how things had gone with Emmett. Allen had been right. This was just what Mama Meg's needed.

7

Making Cuts

Scott was silent on the ride from John's office as Jack drove to Scott's apartment complex. Jack pulled into one of the too-small parking spots in front of Scott's apartment even though he realized Scott would probably ding his door on the car next to them when he got out. Then again, that might be the least of his worries considering what he was about to tell him.

"Well, I guess I should thank you for the ride." Scott's voice trailed off with just the slightest hint of apology.

Jack let the silence become uncomfortable, waiting to see if there was more.

"I know . . ." Scott started. He sighed, seemed to gather his thoughts, and continued, "I screwed up, Jack. I know that. You know I like to have fun, but driving drunk . . . I don't know what I was thinking. I am sorry. I know you probably don't think I am. But I am. I'm sorry I had to put you through all this shit."

"I'm glad you understand what a big deal this is," Jack replied.

Scott dipped his head into his hands, then ran them through his hair. "I do! But damn, Jack. Why do you always have to talk to me like I'm a child?"

Confused, Jack replayed what he thought was a perfectly benign sentence in his head.

"You're always so *condescending*. You're my older brother. Not my father."

Jack didn't take the bait. There was more to this conversation than rehashing old family dynamics. "Drunk driving is a huge deal, Scott, and I would expect you to say the same thing to me if roles were reversed." He tried to stay calm, remembering he needed to be both brother *and* CEO at this moment. "I don't mean to be condescending, but dammit, Scott, you aren't exactly showing me you can make good decisions."

"I don't have time for one of your speeches," Scott declared, swinging open the Land Rover's door and hitting the adjacent car. "I'm outta here."

"Hang on!" Jack said, laying his hand on his shoulder. "Give me a second. No speeches, I promise."

Scott stopped, halfway out of the car, reconsidered, and sat back down. He pulled the door closed, but kept his hand on the handle. Neither of them said anything for what seemed like minutes. Finally Scott spoke. "Listen, I know this whole buyout plan is not what you want to happen."

"That's the understatement of the year."

"But you have to understand . . . I know you're going to land on your feet. You and Laura. You'll be fine. But me? Face it, Jack, I've got nothing. A college dropout, screw-up who still doesn't know where, or if, he fits in, and now you can add convicted felon to my list."

"They're charging you with a misdemeanor, Scott, and you know it."

"The point is, Mom's money is all I have. Can't you see that?"

And now I'm about to fire you, Jack thought, the guilt starting to weigh him down like a load of bricks on his back.

"I'm waiting a year, and I think that is more than fair. If you are able to improve the company enough to buy Brig and me out, don't you think that's, like, a win-win? We get our money and Mama Meg's is more bad-ass than before. Right?"

"How can you say that like you're doing me a favor? Do you have any idea what your back room machinations have gotten me?" The heavy load of guilt he'd felt a moment before began to drop away, brick by brick. And Jack was just getting warmed up. "I lie awake at night filled with worry about how I'm going to keep Mama Meg's from being consumed by Oven Love. Instead of organically growing into a larger, more profitable company on our own timetable, everything is now in panic mode. Decisions I could have taken days to make need to be made instantly. I don't have time to make sure I'm getting things right. I have to hope and pray and make an offering to any deity who will have me! That's my life, man. That's what your *'fairness'* has gotten me."

"You still don't get it," Scott declared.

"Here's what I don't get," Jack said through gritted teeth, trying to hold back the flood of words that threatened to gush out. "You've had nearly three years in IT to prove yourself."

"Oh, here we go," Scott said, shaking his head with disgust.

"Just listen to me." Jack knew there was very little keeping Scott from bolting. "You don't have to be a tech guy if it's not your thing. I got you a job in that department so you could make a regular paycheck—see what that kind of stability brought to your life."

"*You* got me that job because Mom told you to. Period."

Jack wouldn't be sidetracked. "We both thought it would be good for you, that somehow you would be inspired, even if IT wasn't your thing, to find something you did love—something that made you happy and you could be passionate about."

"You just wanted me out of your hair."

"Have you found the job inspiring, Scott?"

Scott huffed. "Hardly."

Jack only half-listened while Scott rambled on about his idiotic co-workers, the crushing monotony of the job, and Gordon always demanding that he do things faster, as if everything was critically urgent. The other part of his mind imagined the conversation that he would have had with his mother about firing Scott. Would she have understood? Would she have forgiven him? *Dammit!* he thought. *I'm the CEO. Not Mom.*

"Scott, you're fired."

Scott's tirade came to a halt. "What?"

"You're beyond hating your job. You're actively doing things to undermine the whole department. The fact that you're the CEO's brother and getting away with everything you do is crushing the morale of the whole department, and I can't have it."

"You're firing your brother."

"I am."

Silence hung between them. A car crept past, searching the lot for a parking spot. The dull, pounding bass of speakers, probably cranked up to eleven, momentarily filled Jack's Land Rover with a tribal beat that reminded him of a headhunter's war chant, or the throbbing pulse that comes right before Jaws attacks.

Like a shot, Scott threw open the door. Jack heard the crash of dented metal on the car parked next to them. Scott got out, slammed the door, and this time, Jack didn't call him back.

Jack pulled out of the apartment complex and headed back to the office. As bad as he felt about firing Scott, Jack knew that he had a lot of work to do to get the company back on solid ground.

* * *

"Have you got a minute?" Jack asked, knocking on the doorframe to Walt's office. Walt nodded and motioned him in. "I want you to meet Tom Tseng."

Walt extended his hand to Tom and pumped it twice. "So, you're our interim CIO," he said with genuine warmth. "You sure you're ready for this?"

"If I'm not, I'll find out soon enough," Tom said with a quick chuckle. "I'm looking forward to working with you and everyone else."

"Tom's worked with Emmett and has done this kind of thing for fourteen years," Jack said. "Emmett had nothing but good things to say about him."

"Well, good. I'm guessing your first order of business will be to evaluate our ERP system?"

"Actually," Tom answered, "I'm going to add that to a list of projects that need prioritizing by the Governance Committee."

"Surely the figuring out the efficacy of our current system would take highest priority," Walt said. "I think everyone would agree. Why waste time talking about it when we can just start?"

"Part of the role of the Governance Committee is to understand what all the needs are from each department and to prioritize them all. That way we can all be sure we're working on what is most important and can allocate resources accordingly."

"I know it might seem counterproductive to have a meeting about something we probably already agree on, but the project is much more than just a simple evaluation. It's going to require some organization," Jack said.

"Seems like we never used to waste so much time in meetings," Walt said, almost as an aside.

"Once we get going, Walt, the process will become very efficient. But we do need to get the process started and that takes some time," Tom said. "Smaller companies can get by with fewer meetings, but Mama Meg's is poised to make a growth spurt. You wouldn't expect a size ten pair of shoes to be effective or comfortable once you're a size eleven, right?"

"I see where you're going with this," Walt said, but Tom didn't take the hint and kept going.

"Sometimes new shoes are a bit uncomfortable until you break them in. And we always miss that old, worn-in, comfortable pair, even though our big toe sticks out through a hole. Soon enough, though, when you get used to the new shoes, you can't imagine going back to the old."

"Alright, fine." This time it was Walt who chuckled. "I'll stop complaining. Just promise me you won't make any more shoe analogies."

"Ha, ha! I promise."

As they left Walt's office, Tom said, "We should really go over the list of projects we will be discussing at the Governance Committee meeting next week. Do you have some time now?"

"Now would be great," Jack replied, finding the nearest empty room and ducking in. It happened to be the visitor room, where all factory tours started and ended.

There were large photos on the wall of Margaret and Jack as the company's former and current CEOs. There were smaller pictures of Laura, Scott and Brigitte. One showed the first delivery truck from sometime in the '70s with the driver waving happily from the cab window. There were informational pictures that chronicled the growth of the company, and even a recreation of Margaret's first kitchen, complete with the original oven and avocado-colored Formica countertops, where it all started. Best of all, there were free samples.

Jack grabbed a package of peanut butter cookies and threw them at Tom. "There won't be another tour for at least thirty minutes. Will that be enough time?"

"Perfect," Tom said, stuffing a cookie into his mouth. "Mmm, these are good!"

"One of the perks of working here." Jack smiled and tossed him three more packages, in rapid succession.

Tom moved faster than Jack would have thought and caught all but the last one, which conveniently dropped right into his lap. "Great. I'll probably gain twenty pounds before I'm done. My wife's not going to be happy."

"Hey, I can take those back if you want." Jack smiled, holding out his hand.

Tom shoved another cookie into his mouth and chewed a few times before a barely intelligible, "It's okay." He finished chewing, swallowed and said, "I'll jog, or shh-umpthing." A few crumbs sputtered out of his mouth and across the table.

Jack laughed. Tom looked more like the type of guy who enjoyed popcorn and a movie rather than a couple hours at the gym. He couldn't imagine him running, even if he were being chased. "Sounds like a plan." He didn't try to keep the sarcasm from his voice.

Tom shot him a sideways grin. "First day on the job and you can already see right through me." He adjusted himself in his chair and Jack could see him switching gears. "Okay, let's talk projects and governance. My first question is who did you put on the Governance Committee?"

"After talking with Emmett, I decided that, given the criticality of what we're doing, the committee had to be made up of the executive team plus Gordon and you." Jack replied.

"That's great! That means that we'll have all the key stakeholders represented when we have to make some hard decisions about project priorities" said Tom as he pushed the cookies aside and pulled out Emmett's report from a couple of weeks back. "One of the things that will have to be a priority will be outsourcing IT infrastructure support so Gordon and his team can focus on the things that are really important to growing the company. I understand you had to let someone in IT go recently?"

"Yeah. You could say that." Jack winced remembering Scott's rage.

"So we're already down in personnel. That's bad news and good news. The bad news is that creates more work for the already tapped-out IT department. The good news? You can use the salary you're no longer paying that person to offset the cost of outsourcing your desktop support and network management."

"That's good," Jack agreed, even though he felt a pang of guilt when he considered his brother as nothing more than a line on a balance sheet. Scott had screwed up, but he was more to Jack than a salary paid or saved. He steeled himself and refocused on what Tom was saying.

"We'll want to have your IT Manager—Gordon, is it?— involved in this project from the start. He and his team need to get out of the infrastructure management business and focus on applications that are critical to running this company. We're probably looking at doing an ERP upgrade or replacement and we need Gordon and his team focused on making that transition as smooth as possible. I can discuss this a little more at the meeting."

"It sounds like we need to get the outsourcing going as soon as possible, then."

"The sooner, the better. I'll work with Gordon to get a Managed Services Provider in place so we can transfer help desk and network admin functions away from your IT team. Only then can we transform the way IT services are delivered. They'll be higher value services and IT will be a major contributor to the success of Mama Meg's."

"Just let me know what you need and I'll get it for you," Jack said. This was real. Change was happening and Jack felt a surge of excitement at the thought. Or maybe it was nerves? He was giving up control over a part of his business. It was a small part, to be sure, but still very important. That was certainly something to be nervous about. Jack thought for a minute and then decided: He was excited.

* * *

Saturday morning was not when Jack wanted to be on a business call, but he had to talk to Allen when Allen was available. "How are things going?" he asked. "How did Emmett work out for you?"

"Great," Jack answered, trying to shake the cobwebs out of his head and the cotton out of his mouth. He'd expected the five a.m. call, but it was still a challenge to convince his body to get up to speed. "Emmett was great. We're just beginning to implement some of his recommendations."

"Governance Committee?" Allen queried, the sounds of horns honking and sitar music playing in the background.

"Yes, and we've brought on an interim CIO. He's been meeting with everyone individually and getting things going with the Governance Committee."

"Any pushback?" A male voice in the background shouted something in a language Jack didn't understand.

"The first Governance Committee meeting got a little heated. Leslie and Chris went back and forth over whose projects were more important. The CIO was able to get a handle on it, though."

"Good. You've got your IT Manager there, too—what's his name?"

"Gordon."

"Yes, Gordon. Make sure he's a part of this whole process. He may be able to step into the CIO role once you're done with your interim guy." Allen's voice got muffled for a minute and it sounded like he was talking to someone else. "Sorry," he said. "I just had to pay my taxi driver."

"Where are you?"

"New Delhi, at least for the next hour or so. Just about to catch a flight to Jakarta." Allen thanked his driver, then resumed his conversation with Jack. "So tell me," he asked, "how did your CIO get control of your team in that first meeting, when Leslie and Chris were arguing?"

"Well," Jack started, "everyone was insisting that their department's needs were the greatest, each making a case for why. Tom—that's our CIO—had some instruction for how the Governance Committee was supposed to operate, but mostly just listened. I thought he'd lost the room. But, after everyone settled down, he clicked through to the next slide on his PowerPoint and showed his list of projects each department had talked to him about earlier in the week. At first it looked like there were only about ten on the list, but then he scrolled down and there were ten more. And he just kept scrolling and scrolling. There must have been seventy individual projects."

"I bet that got their attention."

"You could have heard a pin drop. Once they saw this laundry list, I think they realized there is no way everything will be able to get done and that, for the good of Mama Meg's, some things are going to have to be tabled for now."

"Sounds like you all have your work cut out for you." Allen's voice got muffled again and Jack thought he heard him order some kind of curry. "What about your brother and sister? Are they behaving?"

"I had to fire Scott. That didn't go well."

"I can imagine."

"Other than that, we're still on the same deadline to try and buy them both out or lose the company to Oven Love."

"You've still got eleven months," Allen said. "But better than that, now you've got a plan."

* * *

The conference room was already charged with tension when Jack walked in. Tom was there, setting up for the Governance Committee meeting. But it was Leslie, Chris and Laura who were already starting to defend their department's projects.

"These meetings just keep getting more and more fun," Marcia said with sarcasm as she came in and took a seat. "I hope we're not going to sit here and argue the whole time. I have lots of other things I could be doing."

"The process is a little painful at first," Tom admitted. "This kind of discussion is normal, and necessary to get priorities set." He seemed unfazed by Marcia's attitude and the feeling in the room.

"That's right," Chris said as he was suddenly tuned in to Tom. "And we can't set priorities without a little compromise, can we?" Then turning back to Leslie, "You act like Sales is the most important department in the whole company."

"Well, if we didn't sell, you wouldn't have anything to make." Leslie's smile was insincere, as if she were trying to cover up the acid in her voice, but only making a weak effort. "So, yeah. Sales is the most important. We're the ones moving the product and bringing in the money."

Chris muttered a string of Spanish curse words that fooled no one.

"Before we get too far along," Tom said, "let's take this one potential project at a time." The room miraculously settled and turned their attention to the front.

If Jack had any reservations about Tom's ability to keep his team on task, they were completely erased now. Maybe it was because he was the new guy that everyone was more responsive to him, but Jack didn't care. Things were getting done. He sat back and smiled as Tom dimmed the lights and put up his first slide.

"You remember our to-do list from the last meeting?" There were nods and someone mumbled something under their breath. "I took each department's top three projects and expanded on each one. For example, here's the CRM software Sales needs."

The slide for the CRM project outlined the cost, risk, and benefit to Mama Meg's. It included resource availability and capability as well. Tom had clearly done his homework. The next slide detailed the same information for an integrated SCADA system, and after that, the upgrading of the ERP system. Tom went through about twenty slides and then passed around the same information in packets of paper to everyone.

"I don't think anyone will disagree when I say, we can't do everything. We've got to whittle this list down; figure out what we need to do most, and what we can afford to do."

There was a momentary silence, and then Leslie broke it. "If a CRM for Sales is not at the top of the list . . ."

"Here we go again," Chris interrupted.

"It's obvious that without some kind of product profitability reporting, we can't be successful," Walt said.

"No more important than my marketing analysis software package," Marcia said. "We have to know if our campaigns are successful."

"We can't have any of this until we figure out if our ERP system needs a minor update or a major overhaul," Jack said. "Clearly, that has to be our first priority. Once that's done, we'll have a better idea of what kinds of modules we can add."

"What kind of time frame are we looking at on the ERP evaluation?" Laura asked Tom, who had so far just observed while the discussion unfolded.

"That depends. Gordon?" Tom said, glancing over to the IT Manager in the corner, who looked genuinely surprised to be pulled into the discussion. "What kind of manpower can you give to something like this? Do you have people you can spare?"

Gordon cleared his throat. "I can probably find three people to work on it. Would that be enough?"

"That should be enough for the evaluation phase. We're going to need more than that as we ramp up more projects. And besides, IT will be a major resource for getting all these modules up and running, as well as taking care of training and troubleshooting. They need to be involved at this level and going forward. That's why outsourcing some of the more mundane IT tasks is so important," Tom said. He turned to Walt and said, "How many people can you spare?"

Walt looked a little dumbfounded. "This is an IT project not an accounting project."

"The primary users won't be IT," Tom answered. "IT isn't involved in the day-to-day operations of accounting, so your people are the ones that'll have to tell IT what they do and how they do it as well as what could be done better. They are what we call Subject Matter Experts, SMEs for short." Tom turned to the rest of the group. "Each of you will have to commit resources to this kind of project because each of you has a stake in a successful outcome. IT can help pull together the requirements and document them, but only you and your people know what those requirements should be."

At that, the room erupted back into arguments over different projects' importance. Tom let it play out for a minute or two and then said, "Let's start by eliminating the least important things first. I think we will find that the more important projects will naturally rise to the top. Let's also remember that the important projects are the ones that have the most impact on the strategies that you have developed to meet the company's goals. You should ask yourself three questions about each project. First, how does this project align to company objectives and strategies? Second, do you have the resources to successfully complete this project? Finally is there a significant risk to the company that this project will help to mitigate?"

The tactic worked and four projects were immediately tabled. "We're not eliminating these forever," Tom reminded them. "We're just trying to get a good idea of what we can and should do *now*."

The process continued until there were ten projects everyone could agree were the most important and the meeting was adjourned. As the team filed out of the room, Jack stayed behind. "I'm impressed that you got everyone to whittle the list down, but it's still too big. There's no way we have enough resources to tackle all of these right now," he said to Tom.

"One step at a time." Tom smiled. "The important thing is getting everyone to understand *why* we have to pick and choose. Once they understand what is actually doable, and what is best for the company as a whole, they'll get behind the projects. We need each department to be fully committed to reaching the desired outcome."

"So, how are you going to break it to them—that we still have to let some of these projects go for now?"

"We've got our list prioritized. Next time we meet, we will look at it against our budget and resource availability and a line will have to be drawn somewhere."

"They're not going to be happy when you tell them," Jack said.

"Oh, it's not going to be me who draws the line. The Governance Committee will. They have to. And they will—once they see the numbers. It's the only way to get everyone to buy into the projects and then go back and sell them to their teams. You'll see. Everything will work out."

"Well, if you can pull it off, you're a better man than me." Jack clapped Tom on the back as they made their way out of the conference room. "Then what?" Jack added. "Where do we go from there?"

"That's when the fun starts," Tom replied. "That's when we start getting things done."

8

Slicing Through Red Tape

Tom Tseng <tomt@traskco.com> April 7

To: Jack McCallister <jackmc@mamamegs.com>
Cc: Governance Committee

Re: Monthly Status Report

Jack:

Great progress at our meeting. Totally normal to have a bit of chaos as things get off the ground but before you know it, the team will be a well-oiled machine.

Just a quick recap of the decisions and action items:

- Keep current ERP with updates and additional modules for CRM and MRP
- SCADA interface modules were identified
- Complete ERP implementation project plan – Gordon and Tom
- Establish ERP project implementation team – Gordon and Walt

We've set up short deadlines for each phase so we can move through the ERP implementation as quickly as possible. It's aggressive, but we should be able to handle it.

I'll keep everyone updated.

Tom Tseng | CIO Consultant | **Trask Consulting**

MOBILE: 971.555.5254

"I talked to Brigitte this morning." Laura had walked into Jack's office without even knocking and sat down in the chair across the desk from him. She leaned back, folded her arms and stared, as if she was waiting for a specific reply.

Jack didn't know what he was supposed to say. "Okay," he tried. "What did she want?"

"Scott has moved in with her." She sounded just a bit incredulous that he hadn't somehow known this.

"Thanks for letting me know?" Jack tried.

"Jack! Scott lost his place. He has nowhere to go."

"I thought you said he was at Brigitte's."

"You know what I mean." She stood up and started pacing the room. "He has no income, no way to pay for rent; he can't live with Brigitte forever!"

"Maybe he could move in with you?" Jack offered jokingly.

"Ugh!" Laura threw her hands up in the air and sank back into the chair.

"Listen," Jack said. "I know you're worried about Scott, but he'll be fine. He's been bailed out or handed on a silver platter everything he's ever done in his life. It will be good for him to have to figure this out on his own—maybe give him a little confidence."

"You think Scott lacks confidence?"

"He does when it comes to his ability to do things for himself," Jack replied. He knew his mother had loved Scott, but he never had to work for anything; never had to suffer the consequences of his actions. How was he supposed to know what he was capable of if he never had to stand on his own two feet? "You'll see."

"I don't know how you can be so calm about this. Aren't you worried even a little bit?"

"What? That he'll call and ask me for money? Sure I am." Jack laughed at his own joke.

"No, that he'll end up homeless, living in a shelter, or worse, under a bridge!"

Jack laughed. "You know Scott is resourceful enough to keep a roof over his head. Look! He's already got one with Brigitte. See? He'll be fine."

Laura sighed in resignation and rubbed her temples. "I know. I know you're right. I just can't help worrying."

"Listen," Jack said trying to comfort her, "I know it's hard to see Scott flounder a bit, but it's the best thing for him. Besides, if you want something to worry about, worry about what Leslie's going to say when she finds out she's not getting her E-Sales software."

"What? Why not? She's been completely obnoxious about it, but she's done her homework, Jack. She needs some kind of software to bring her team up to speed."

"She's definitely getting something. It just won't be what she wants. Tom said our ERP vendor looked over our requirements list and pointed out that we already have some sales tracking capabilities built into the system. We've even been paying maintenance on it every year. We just didn't know it was there or how to use it."

"Will it have everything she wants? Maybe she won't be as upset as you think?"

"We're a few versions behind, but once we get the updates, it should be pretty close to what she's looking for with E-Sales. It just won't have the cloud-based reporting, so she won't be able to find out what her sales people are doing in real time."

"Sticking with what we've already got should save time," Laura offered. "Most everyone is somewhat familiar with the system, so it makes sense to use what we've already got. Surely Leslie will be able to see that as a good thing, right?"

"And it saves us some money so we can get additional modules for other departments. Because we're sticking with the system we've got, with updates, this re-implementation will take three or four months instead of six to nine. It makes a huge difference."

"It sounds great. So is it a done deal?"

"We need to run it through the Governance Committee and get a vote. I don't see why everyone won't agree to it . . . or at least the majority." He arched his brows knowingly and she nodded. Leslie was not going to be happy.

* * *

"You want me to give up E-Sales so we can have another module for Chris's department?" Leslie asked, hands clenched, her voice thick with sarcasm.

"The sales component currently on the ERP system has nearly everything you're looking for with E-Sales. It will integrate with the rest of the system easily and quickly," Tom answered. "We can revisit getting E-Sales later, but right now, to just get up and running, I think sticking with what we've got is the best plan."

"Makes sense to me," Walt said with confidence, then shrank into his chair when Leslie glared at him.

"You know we're under a lot of pressure. The clock is ticking," Jack declared. "We need all the time we can get if we're going to be able to keep the company."

"That's right," Tom said, backing him up. God bless him. Jack wondered if they were paying him enough. "What we're looking at is an upgrade and re-implementation of our current ERP system so everyone is trained on how to use it effectively. Then we will add the modules. I'll work with the vendor and help coordinate the training here with people from each department. It's the fastest way to get up and running."

"If we get going on this now," Jack said, "it should take us about ninety days until we are trained and all the modules are in place."

"If you were going with a brand new system," Tom added, "it would be more like a year before everything was in place and people were up to speed."

"And we don't have that kind of time," Chris agreed.

"Exactly." Jack looked around the room and could see everyone understood the importance of moving forward together with this project. Even Leslie seemed resigned to the idea, but the vacant look in her eyes made it obvious she wasn't happy about it. She knew they were desperate for quick solutions.

"It might just be a formality, but let's take a vote?" Tom said. "All in favor of moving forward with the upgrade . . ."

Jack's hand shot up, followed by Laura's, Walt's, Chris's, Gordon's and Marcia's. Leslie looked at those seated around the table as if they had betrayed her, then reluctantly raised her hand. "Yeah, I get it," she muttered. "I don't like it, but I get it."

"Great," Tom said. "We'll get started on it right away." Then turning to Gordon he said, "Why don't you stay behind so we can talk about what our next steps are."

Gordon nodded.

"Mind if I listen in, too?" Jack asked as people gathered up their things and exited the conference room. He'd noticed that Leslie had been the first one to leave without saying a word to anyone. She was mad, but she would get over it. After all, she had voted to move forward with the current sales module. She just needed time to blow off some steam.

In the meantime, Jack wanted to hear how the ERP roll-out was going to happen, both so he could know what to expect and how he could help things move along. But that wasn't all. He was also curious to see how Gordon was coming along. He ran the IT department with skill and determination. He worked well under pressure and was meticulous with his own work and required the same from his team. But did he have what it took to be an executive?

"Great," Tom said. "It will be great for you to hear how we're going to do this because this model should be used going forward for all projects." He pulled a couple papers from a folder in front of him and handed one to Gordon and one to Jack. "Gordon, we can't just let this project flounder. It has to move along at the most efficient rate. To do that requires a certain type of organization."

Gordon nodded, and pulled out a pen to take notes.

"The first step in successful project implementation is a Governance Committee, and we can check that off our list. But beyond that, we need to have a project steering team that will make sure the ERP upgrade is going smoothly and deadlines are being met. They'll report to the Governance Committee."

Gordon wrote a few things on his paper, then asked, "Who will the team be made up of?"

"Someone from the Executive team should sponsor it. In this case, it makes sense for that person to be me, since the ERP upgrade is a company-wide project. But you will also be part of the team, as IT Manager. In fact, I think you should be the project manager."

Gordon looked up from his note-taking, the uncertainty visible on his face. "Surely they've told you about the last project I tried to manage." Gordon looked at Jack as if wanting confirmation, but Jack stayed silent and let Tom do the talking.

"The reason that project failed was because you didn't have this kind of organization." Tom tapped the sheet in front of him. "Before, you didn't have guidelines or methods to managing projects and the results were always mixed. It wasn't just you either. Many of the projects undertaken in the last few years, even the ones that were considered 'successful,' have failed to deliver the full possible value to Mama Meg's. It's been hit-and-miss. That's not how we're going to do it this time."

Gordon nodded his head. "Okay. I'm in." Jack noticed Gordon sat up a little straighter in his seat as if some unseen force had just bestowed him with an extra measure of confidence.

"Great. We will also need managers who have a stake in this project on the team as well. Jack?" Tom was on a roll, ticking off the items on some mental list like someone who'd done this a few times before. "Will you get Walt, Marcia, Leslie and Chris to dedicate a department manager to this team?"

Jack nodded and pulled out his phone to take care of it right then.

Turning back to Gordon, Tom continued, "They will help us gain cooperation from each of the departments so the roll-out can happen efficiently. Together, we will set the direction for the project, make sure that resources are allocated correctly, while monitoring the progress and the budget."

"Okay. What about the project implementation team?" Gordon asked, pointing to the last heading on Tom's list.

"You'll lead that team, which will be made up of people from IT, as well as the SMEs from each department. This is where stuff gets done. You'll be on the front lines, getting the functional requirements and taking recommendations from the vendor. You'll be responsible to see that testing is done and to making sure the system works as it should. There will need to be a post-project review and you and the implementation team will also be responsible for that."

"It sounds like we've got our work cut out for us." Gordon sat back in his chair, his eyes wide, looking a little overwhelmed.

"I'll be here to guide and mentor you along the way." Tom's voice was reassuring and confident. "Once you have these guidelines in place, any project can be run successfully."

"Do you need anything else from me?" Jack asked.

"Your support has been invaluable. Having someone like me come in and stir things up—change the status quo—can be disruptive. When the CEO is fully on board, like you've been, it makes things go much more smoothly." Tom smiled as he gathered up his things. "Keep doing that and I'll let you know if Gordon and I need anything else."

* * *

Tom Tseng <tomt@traskco.com>   May 8

To: Jack McCallister <jackmc@mamamegs.com>
Cc: Governance Committee

Re: Monthly Status Report

Jack:

Here's a quick summary of the ERP implementation plan we hacked out at this week's meeting:

- Phase 1: Planning and organization – Complete!
- Phase 2: Configuration & Modeling – Complete!
- Phase 3: Testing – In Progress
- Phase 4: Training
- Phase 5: Go Live Planning & Execution
- Phase 6: GO-LIVE after month-end close

We're meeting our deadlines, which is great. Everyone has stepped up to make this project happen and that is the most important ingredient for success. We're also staying on track by breaking up some of the bigger phases into smaller, more manageable chunks.

Action items we discussed for the IT Governance Committee:

- Support moratorium on reports, patches, development in the current ERP System

- Curtail other projects competing for resources, time and attention
- Enable key users time to map business processes, train and test

Let me know if you have any questions or issues. Otherwise, onward!

Tom Tseng | CIO Consultant | **Trask Consulting**

MOBILE: 971.555.5254

Jack sat down at his desk after a long weekend. It had felt great to be able to take a day off and spend it with his family. Five months ago, taking a day off would have seemed laughable with how busy things had been at Mama Meg's. Jack realized now, as he saw how well the ERP upgrade was being handled by Gordon and Tom, that his business hadn't been directed. They'd been unfocused and for all the extra hours they were putting in, their results didn't reflect much progress. They'd been floundering.

He straightened the photo of him and his family on the desk, then looked at the walls of his office. They were still lined with promotional posters featuring his mother: Meg pulling a baking sheet full of chocolate chip cookies out of the oven; Meg packing cookies into the lunches of child actors with too-big smiles; Meg taking a bite out of a snickerdoodle with the tagline, "For the Love of Cookies."

Maybe it's time for an update, Jack thought. It felt to him like Mama Meg's had definitely turned a corner and was now becoming a bigger, stronger company and, in a way, leaving the old ways behind. Margaret McCallister created a beloved regional brand. Now Jack was going to make that brand a national best-seller.

He reflected on the progress over the last few months: they were halfway into the ERP system update and everything had been going well. Jack realized, though, that with the Governance Committee having hit their stride, luck had nothing to do with their success. After those first few contentious meetings, he'd wondered if they'd ever be able to come together to work efficiently. But they had. Now, instead of defending their departmental needs, everyone had a more holistic approach and their discussions always focused on what was best for the whole company. *It's funny*, Jack thought. *The thing that is best for the company as a whole, usually ends up having the most benefit to the individual departments as well.* For the first time since he could remember, it seemed like everyone was moving together toward the same goal. It felt right.

Jack looked at his calendar. Everything seemed to be on track for their ninety-day completion deadline. He still wasn't sure how they were going to be able to pay out Scott and Brigitte, but he had time. He would think of something.

Jack heard a light knock and looked up to see Laura standing in his doorway. "You got a minute?" she inquired. "I want to run some numbers past you."

"Sure," Jack replied, clearing a spot off on his desk for Laura to lay out whatever spreadsheets she'd brought along. But when she took a seat, she didn't pull out any paper. She didn't even have her laptop.

Laura was aware of Jack's confusion, but just smiled.

"So what do you want to show me?" he queried.

"They're on your computer . . . on the ERP. Just log in." The corner of Laura's mouth twitched as she tried to hold back her grin, just a little too smug, in Jack's opinion.

"Oh, right. The ERP." Jack wondered how much longer it would take before he'd forget about those migraine-inducing spreadsheets.

"The information is still not perfect, but it's getting there," she said with a smile.

Jack was looking over the R&D report when Walt stuck his head into Jack's office. "Jack," he said with a little annoyance, "what's this I hear about Leslie buying E-Sales for her team? I thought we'd agreed to wait for that."

"What?" Jack exclaimed, his brow knit in confusion. "What are you talking about?"

"Leslie went ahead and bought that sales program she's been whining about for the last few months," Walt repeated. "If she's just going to do whatever she wants, what's the point of having a Governance Committee?"

Jack was already out of his chair and had pushed past Walt, but could hear him ask, "Do you know how much money she spent . . . ?" as he rounded the corner. Jack didn't care how much she'd spent—it was her going against the decision of the Committee that had his blood pressure rising—but Walt's question suddenly made him assume the worst.

Jack fumed as he wondered what Leslie could possibly be thinking. They'd all agreed to wait. Didn't she understand the importance in being united on the ERP project? Each step closer to Leslie's office, his temper seethed as the angry speech he planned to unleash on her started to take shape. Leslie had been a hindrance at every turn. Why was she the one who always had to be managed and placated, like a diva? He needed his executives to act in the best interest of the whole company. It seemed like Leslie was only interested in doing things that benefited just her and the Sales department.

As he rounded the corner he nearly plowed into Tom.

"Jack, I was just coming to find you," Tom said. His shirt looked a little more rumpled than usual and beads of sweat were starting to break out on his forehead, as if he'd been running. "It appears Leslie has . . ." Tom panted, slightly out of breath.

"I heard," Jack practically growled.

"I just got done talking to her." Tom paused to look at his beeping phone and then pushed a button to silence it. "It's Marcia. Pretty sure she wants to yell at me about Leslie, too. I can call her back later." He shoved his phone back in his pocket and said, "I'm guessing you're on your way to talk to her?"

Jack glared in response.

"Why don't you let me fill you in on everything first."

"Fine," Jack huffed. "This wasn't how it was supposed to go."

"I know this is frustrating."

"I'm beyond frustration, Tom."

"If it makes you feel any better, I've rarely had a roll-out go perfectly. There are always bumps in the road. I'm used to working through them."

"This isn't a bump," Jack fumed. "This feels more like a spike strip . . . and Leslie laid it out herself."

"It's not quite that bad." Tom's breathing was returning to normal and his voice had an air of practiced calm. Jack found it incredibly annoying. He directed Jack into an open conference room and closed the door behind them. They sat down and Tom continued. "Yes, you're right that Leslie screwed up," he said as a vein in Jack's forehead started to bulge. "But of all the Sales systems Leslie could have picked, she picked one that will integrate with our ERP. So all we have to do is implement that integration."

Jack resisted the urge to pound the table, but kept listening.

"If she had purchased a lesser-known system, we would have had to build something specific to integrate it into the ERP. It would have taken months. But because it is compatible, it will take very little time to get it to the point where we can move data back and forth. It will actually be very good."

Jack wasn't ready to calm down yet. "I don't care that she picked the perfect program! She went against what we all had agreed on! She's undermined the trust of the Committee. How are we supposed to work together when Leslie is essentially flipping the bird to the rest of the Governance Committee?"

"Leslie's major gripe was that the current sales program in the ERP system was more batch oriented: it didn't give her data in real time. The cloud service provider she's going with can do that, and the cost is not that much more than what we were paying for the current sales module."

Jack felt his heart rate start to drop, but his sense of justice was just kicking in. "But we agreed!" Jack huffed. "We all voted. She was still getting something better than what she had before." Jack closed his eyes and shook his head slowly back and forth, still not believing Leslie could have done something like this. "I suppose there will be training for her team that will take them off-site, and even more downtime as we try to integrate it. This is going to throw off our timeline, isn't it?"

"Actually," Tom said, "it's not going to push us back too much. Her program came with training. If we'd stuck with our ERP's sales package, we would have had to train everyone. Now her people will get that training from the software company. In a way, it's like we are replacing one task with another."

"But it will push us back?" Jack asked, still not ready to give in.

"Yes," Tom admitted. "But only about two weeks."

Jack stared at the wall. *Two weeks,* he thought. He was five months into his year . . . the year before he would lose his company. Two weeks may not have sounded like a lot to Tom, and they clearly didn't to Leslie, but to Jack, it felt like a punch in the throat. Didn't Leslie realize how high the stakes were? Didn't she care?

"But that's not all that is going to benefit us," Tom continued. "We can pull all the data she's collecting back into the ERP system. It will help Production, Marketing, Finance, Research and Development . . . everyone. Plus, the data from the ERP system that is coming from all the other departments can get pushed back out to her sales people. They'll be more effective in the field because they'll have more information than ever."

"It sounds like you're justifying what she's done," Jack countered, still too upset to look Tom in the eye.

"Leslie went behind everyone's backs. She shouldn't have done it." Tom leaned forward in his chair, resting his arms on his knees. "It would have been better if she had just gone with our original plan to use the program we already had and not bought the service."

Jack finally looked at Tom.

"But," Tom said, "we can deal with it. We will take what good out of it we can and deal with the rest."

"Walt's freaking out about the cost."

"I will talk to Walt."

"Leslie can't just get away with this. She needs to know how much she has potentially hurt Mama Meg's."

"She's going to talk to you about that. I told her she at least owes you an explanation and apology."

Jack was still fuming, although his emotions swung from anger to hurt. As he was mentally going over all the things he wanted to say to Leslie, Tom's phone started beeping again. "Marcia again?" he asked

"It's Walt, this time," Tom replied. "Well, I better take care of this. I'll touch base with you later today, okay?"

Jack nodded.

"Hi, Walt . . ." Tom's voice trailed off as Jack exited the conference room.

How could one person have so much power to screw things up? Jack wondered, and then his thoughts turned from Leslie to Scott. He hadn't heard from him in several weeks. He remembered his own children, and how their silence at home often meant they were up to trouble. Scott wasn't a little kid. As much as he acted like one. How much more trouble could he get into? *I'm sure there's nothing to worry about,* he thought.

* * *

Jack didn't want to wait for Leslie to come to him, so he went to her. He knocked on the doorframe and she looked up from her desk. "Jack." Her eyes darted from a pile of papers on her desk, to her computer screen, to her wastebasket, but never landed on Jack's own. There was a tinge of emotion to her voice, but Jack wasn't sure if it was regret for her actions or regret for getting caught. "Come in. I guess you've heard about my purchase."

"I have." He took a deep breath and tried to calm himself. "Why does it feel like you're undermining everything I've been working for, Leslie? Why does it feel like you're working against me? You realize that because of your actions, we might not even have a company in seven months?"

"I know it feels like that now, Jack."

"You have no idea what I'm feeling. You want to know what I'm feeling? Betrayed! How could you do this? You went behind everyone's back after we all agreed on a course of action. We're all making sacrifices. We all are. It's not just you."

"You know I feel strongly about my responsibilities to this company. I want nothing less than for Mama Meg's to dominate the market, Jack. That's my goal. And in case you forgot, it's your goal, too. You're the one who set my sales goals—and they're ambitious. We can reach them, but not without the right tools. The only way I can be competitive is if we have E-Sales."

"Did you even consider how this is going to affect everyone else? Now we all have a delay while we integrate your programs."

"I know," Leslie murmured, head lowered. "I know. But if it had just been part of the project originally, like I wanted . . ."

"You can't go against the group when you don't get what you want. We stick together. We work towards the same goals. What you've done can potentially undermine the work the Governance Committee has been doing. We can't afford to go back to the way we were doing things."

"I agree, but don't you see? This sales program will actually help everyone with more information in real time."

"I realize that. But don't *you* see? What you've done could put the whole company's future in jeopardy."

There was a long silence and then Leslie said apologetically, "I'm sorry, Jack. I was wrong. But I just didn't know another way to get this program into the hands of my sales people. I tried going through the right channels."

"Everyone is pretty upset about this, you know," Jack replied.

"So I've heard." Leslie looked down at her hands, folded in her lap. Was she actually feeling remorse? "I'll talk to them. I'll make sure they know I'm committed."

"You better be. I can't keep wondering if you're trying to help Mama Meg's or hurt it. One more time I have to question your loyalty and I'll need to find someone else to run my sales department."

"Jack, believe me. I'm completely loyal to Mama Meg's. No one wants to kick Oven Love's ass more than me."

Jack thought back to Leslie's connection with Oven Love's COO, Soren. Was it just a sense of competition with her old college boyfriend that was motivating her actions? Or was there something else going on?

* * *

Jack felt drained, but the day wasn't even halfway over yet. He wondered if he'd done the right thing by not firing Leslie, but quickly realized now was not the time to bring in a new executive. They just needed to get through the upgrade and re-implementation and then he could worry about what to do with Leslie.

The phone rang and Jack recognized the number of their company and family lawyer. "John!" he said with as much warmth as he could muster. "How are you doing?" Jack hadn't talked to him since Scott's DUI incident several months back.

"I'm okay, but I've got some news you're not going to be happy with," he said.

"Oh, John, I don't think I can take much more today."

"Well, you're going to find out sooner or later. Your brother just got a job with Oven Love."

Tom Tseng <tomt@traskco.com>   June 12

To: Jack McCallister <jackmc@mamamegs.com>
Cc: Governance Committee

Re: Monthly Status Report

Jack:

We're in the home stretch!

We've almost completed the ERP training (phase 4) and are getting ready to go live.

Gordon's done a great job keeping his team on task and making deadlines. We need to keep giving the key users the resources to have success with their training and go-live activities, as well as keeping a lid on competing projects.

If we keep going like we have, everyone is going to deserve a huge pat on the back when the ERP is up and running.

Tom Tseng | CIO Consultant | **Trask Consulting**

MOBILE: 971.555.5254

9

A Stab at Reconciliation

The sun beat down on the pavilion and Jack felt drops of sweat roll down his back under his thick polo shirt. Why had he chosen to wear navy blue on what must be the hottest day of the year? From the DJ's tent, he watched as hundreds of Mama Meg's employees and their families played volleyball, filled themselves with hamburgers and macaroni salad, and tried to keep snow cones from dripping down the fronts of their shirts. At the bottom of the hill, kids and adults were in some sort of hula hoop contest. Off in the distance, many had put on their swimsuits and were hurling themselves down a massive slip-and-slide that had to be at least a hundred yards long. Everyone was having a great time. They deserved to.

"You ready for your speech?"

Jack turned to see Chris, who had come up behind him.

"Sure glad it's you and not me," Chris said, shaking his head. "Public speaking is not my thing."

"That's a little hard to believe," Jack replied. "The way you order everyone around on the production floor, I think talking to a crowd would come as second nature to you."

"Sure, I can boss people around. And I've got no problem telling folks when they're screwing up. But you've got to give a speech, my friend." Chris chuckled under his breath as he patted Jack on the shoulder. "All these people are going to be looking at you, waiting for you to say something that will *inspire* them."

He gazed out onto the company picnic that was well into its third hour of fun and games. "There must be at least five hundred people out there. I don't know how that doesn't make you a little nervous."

"Thanks for the pep talk," Jack said, now feeling the tiniest flutter in his stomach. He shook it off. "It's not as hard as you think," reminding himself of this fact at the same time he was trying to convince Chris. "When you have great news to share, it doesn't matter what you say. Everyone's going to love you, right?"

"Good point," Chris admitted and turned as Laura came up to the tent, followed by Walt.

"Brigitte did a good job with this party, don't you think?" Laura asked. "The t-shirt cannon was a nice touch." As she said this, another t-shirt shot into a crowd of people who wildly scrambled to claim it.

"Brigitte and her *team* did a good job," Jack stated. "She had a lot of help."

"And she spent a lot of money," Walt added. "Did you see how much this party went over budget?"

"Surprise, surprise. Walt's complaining about money." Everyone turned around and saw Leslie just stepping under the tent with Marcia.

"Just because we're doing well doesn't mean we should spend irresponsibly," Walt cautioned.

"This party is hardly irresponsible," Marcia chimed in. "It's excellent for employee relations. You know that, Walt."

"If we could have just stayed within the budget . . ."

"Okay, let's not get into this now. The party is perfect and, in my opinion, worth going a little over budget," Jack declared.

Walt grumbled something under his breath that Jack chose to ignore. Despite the heat, it was a great day and the culmination of months of hard work on everyone's part. The upgrade to the ERP had been successful and it appeared Mama Meg's was on track to exceed their sales goals.

Jack saw Tom walking up the hill and knew, once they were all assembled, it would be time for him to speak. He pulled a folded piece of paper out of his back pocket to check his notes once more. Marcia might think of this party as good business sense, but for Jack, it was more like a family reunion. And just like a family reunion, even if he didn't know every single person by their first name, he still knew they belonged to each other.

"It's about time," Leslie exclaimed when Tom ducked under the tent. "What took you so long?"

Tom held up an envelope. "I won the hula hoop contest," he said, grinning and shaking his hips as proof, in case anyone had doubts. "A fifty-dollar gift certificate to Mack's Steakhouse."

"Fifty dollars?" Chris said. "If I'd known that was the prize, I would have entered, too. I could have taken you down. *Easy.*"

"You can't even walk and chew gum at the same time," Laura joked with Chris, laughing. "You think we'd believe you can hula hoop?"

Everyone laughed, except Walt, who was looking stressed and uncomfortable, most likely because someone decided giving a fifty-dollar prize for a hula hoop contest was a good idea.

"You ready?" the DJ asked. "I've got about thirty seconds before this song is over."

Jack nodded.

As the final beats of the music faded away, the DJ thundered, "Mama Meg's employees!" He held the last syllable of the word "employees" like he was an announcer for one of those over-produced, fake wrestling matches. "Who makes the best cookies in all the land?" he asked, thrusting the microphone towards the crowd and cupping his hand to his ear, waiting.

"Mama Meg's!" everyone shouted.

"I can't hear you!"

"Mama Meg's!" came the thundering reply.

"One. More. Time!" he prompted.

Everyone was on their feet. The energy was electric, and when they replied, Jack felt it reverberate in his chest. "Mama Meg's!"

The DJ turned, and held the microphone out to Jack. "It's all yours."

Jack took the mic and looked out on the cheering crowd. Time slowed and he thought back to nine months ago, when he stood in the boardroom with nearly half of the members voting to sell his company. He'd been full of fight, but so unsure about how he was going to win. It had been a hard road, but with Emmett and Tom's help, and ultimately Allen's, Jack had turned things around. The roar reentered his ears and he snapped back into the moment. A rush of gratitude for everyone who made Mama Meg's run filled him and he pronounced, "That's right! We're Mama Meg's and we make the best cookies in the whole world!"

The crowd shouted and hooted, fists pumping in the air.

"Today we might be the strongest regional brand in the area, but soon, we'll show this whole country that premium ingredients, my mother's own secret recipes, and the hardest-working employees anywhere make the best-tasting cookies."

Jack thought he heard Laura say something about "laying it on a little thick," but with all the noise, it was hard to be sure.

"The last four months we've asked a lot of all of you as we've transitioned to a better, sleeker, more responsive ERP system. Your patience through the bumps in the road, and ultimate dedication to making things work, has resulted in a successful update. Already we are beginning to see the benefits in greater efficiency, better communication, and increased sales. And that's in large part because of all of you. So give yourselves a hand!"

Jack waited until the clapping died down. "This party is not only for you, the faithful Mama Meg's employees, but also for your families who have supported your working late a night or two." That understatement generated a laugh, mostly from the production staff, who definitely put in more than one or two late nights, Jack imagined. "Enjoy yourselves, and I, along with my sister Laura," Jack motioned for Laura to step forward, "Leslie, Walt . . . all you guys, come on up, too," he motioned to the rest of them, throwing his arms around the group as they gathered around. "All of us look forward to working with you, as together, we put Mama Meg's on the national map!"

All seven of them stood and clapped with the crowd while, off to the side, someone shot shirt after shirt out of the t-shirt cannon. As the excitement shifted from Jack and his team to the free t-shirts flying through the air, the DJ started up the music again and Jack turned to his team. "All hype aside, we wouldn't be where we are today without each of you. The way you have all come together in the last few months . . . it very well might turn out to be the thing that will save this company."

"Thanks, Jack," Marcia said.

"You mean that, Jack? Even for me?" Leslie inquired. Her tone was mocking but the look on her face revealed some lingering insecurity. "Even though I went rogue and bought E-Sales for my team?"

"You're going to ruin my moment by bringing that up now?" Jack teased.

"Actually," Chris spoke, "the numbers I'm getting from that program make my job so much easier. I never thought I'd admit this to you, Leslie, but I'm glad you went rogue."

"I suppose it worked out," Walt retorted, a little stiffly.

"Oh, come on, Walt," Laura said, chiding. "Just yesterday you were telling me how helpful Leslie's program was when it came to calculating operating projections."

Slowly, Walt's stern face cracked into a smile that widened until it broke into a huge grin. "Fine." Sheepishly he turned to Leslie. "I said it, okay?"

"Walter J. Torbet!" Leslie exclaimed, feigning shock. "You said something nice about me?"

"Actually, it was something nice about your *sales program*," he responded, trying to maintain a dignified look. It didn't last long.

Leslie threw her arms around Walt, who kept his arms uncomfortably at his sides, clearly unsure of where to put them. "Walt, you like me! You really like me!" Leslie trilled.

Marcia was the first to laugh, but soon, everyone else joined in.

"Heads!" someone shouted as a t-shirt dropped out of the air right in front of Walt.

He reached his hands out to grab it and fumbled, stooge-like, as he tried to gain control of the rolled-up shirt. When he finally had it in his grasp, he raised it high above his head, triumphant. Many of the Mama Meg's employees had noticed the scene and cheered loudly.

While Walt was still celebrating his catch, Jack heard the cannon go off again. Another t-shirt arced through the air, heading, again, right for their group. Before he could say anything, the shirt had made a direct hit with Laura's left shoulder.

"Hey! Enough already." Laura laughed off the attack, as Jack followed the trajectory back to its source, squinting to focus in on who was operating the cannon. It didn't take long to realize something wasn't right. It looked like two people were struggling over who was going to shoot.

Jack watched as one guy pointed the cannon in the direction of Jack and his group, ready to launch yet another rolled-up t-shirt their way. At the last minute, the second guy grabbed control of the cannon, knocking the barrel out of line and the prized payload landed safely into a crowd of kids who had been begging for him to shoot their way.

You have got to be kidding me, Jack thought as the scene before him came into focus. He immediately headed towards the cannon operators.

"Jack, what's going on?" Chris asked when he suddenly took off.

Jack said nothing, but slowed down long enough to shoot a look at Laura, who had been laughing over something with Marcia. An unspoken message passed between them and Laura said, "Excuse me," and followed after Jack.

"Do you know how he found out about the picnic?" Jack asked as he took long, angry steps across the grassy field. Laura had to jog to keep up.

"I imagine Brigitte told him. She's been planning this day for a month. I'm sure it would have come up."

"He's an Oven Love employee. He shouldn't be here."

"He's still family, Jack."

"He's attacking us with the t-shirt cannon, *Laura*." Were they really going to debate this now? Scott had wrestled control of the cannon away from the other guy, looked up to see both of them approaching and leveled the cannon right at them, his intention crystal clear. "Don't you dare," Jack growled in Scott's direction.

Laura, still having trouble keeping up with Jack's stride, ran and jumped in front of Jack. "Scott!" She held her arms out at her sides, whether to make herself into a larger target or to indicate everyone should just calm down, Jack didn't know. She must have known that if Jack got a t-shirt to the gut from close range, the party would come to a very awkward, very abrupt end. Luckily, few, if any, people realized what was going on and, from a distance, it could still pass for fun and games.

They were now only twenty feet away from the business end of the cannon that Scott held over his shoulder like a bazooka. The grin on his face revealed nothing: He was either just joking around, or he had completely lost his mind. "Put that stupid thing down." Laura's voice was firm and powerful and in that moment she sounded just like Margaret. How many times had his mother said the same thing to both Scott and Jack over the years?

Scott must have noticed it, too, because his grin flickered for just a moment, before he said, "Guys, lighten up. Isn't this supposed to be a party? I'm just kidding."

Jack started to say something but Laura intervened. "Scott, I'm pretty sure this," she grabbed the t-shirt cannon from his hands and handed it back to its grateful original operator, "is not a toy. You could have hurt someone. Someone might have thought you were trying to hit people on purpose."

The asshole was *doing it on purpose*, Jack thought. *Why is she going so easy on him?* Jack would have wrung his neck first and asked questions later, regardless of the scene it would make. He tried to speak, but again, Laura cut him off.

"Did you just get here? Do you want to grab a plate of food?"

Like hell he's going to eat my food, Jack thought. He tried to step around Laura, but she subtly yet firmly put her hand on his arm: a warning to stay out of it. She would handle this.

Jack hadn't realized how stiff Scott's posture had been until he visibly relaxed at Laura's invitation to eat. "Okay." There was uncertainty in his voice and he looked at Jack, anticipating a protest. When there was none he said, "That sounds good."

Laura stepped towards Scott and pointed him towards the buffet tables. "The burgers are actually pretty good, but I'd skip the macaroni salad," Jack heard her say as they walked off. He was amped from the near confrontation, his heart still pounding in his chest. It was the kind of feeling only a ten-mile run would solve. Either that or more beers than would be appropriate for a family picnic. Neither were good options.

About ten yards off, the t-shirt cannon guy was just opening another box of shirts. Jack eyed the CO_2-powered launcher with curiosity. He knew what he had to do.

"Hey, would you mind?" he asked as he approached, pointing to the cannon. "I promise, I won't aim for anyone."

The t-shirt cannon guy's shoulders slumped a little and he nodded, holding out the cannon for Jack. "Just turn the safety off and pull the trigger," he said.

Jack felt his tension slip away as he launched the shirt high into the air. It felt like it hung there forever. A crowd of people were watching, trying to predict where it would land and jockeying for the best position. Then it plummeted towards earth and came to rest on the roof of the picnic pavilion. "Give me another one," he said to the guy. "This is awesome."

* * *

"I just dropped Scott off." Even over the phone, Jack could tell Laura was exhausted. After they'd gone for some food, Jack hadn't seen either of them for the rest of the day.

"It's nearly nine p.m. Have you been with him this whole time?"

"Yeah. He had a lot to talk about. Things went south for him at Oven Love."

"Well, that's not a surprise. Did they fire him?"

"Yes, but let me start from the beginning." Laura loved a good story almost as much as Jack loved quick facts; bullet-pointed, pithy and succinct. He sighed knowing there was no rushing her.

"Don't worry. I'll try and make it fast," she said. "So, after inane pleasantries . . ."

"Did he tell you what the hell he was doing at our company picnic? Did he mention why he was attacking us with t-shirts?" Jack demanded.

She continued as if she hadn't even heard him. ". . . we talked about his job at Oven Love. He originally reached out to them because he was mad at you for firing him. He might have indicated that he had information on Mama Meg's that would be valuable to them."

"He what?" Jack's mind immediately started thinking of all the things he could have told them before realizing Scott probably didn't know much.

"He was bluffing, of course," Laura continued, "but they hired him as the Director of Competitive Analysis anyway. It took them all this time to realize he had nothing more than what they already knew—that a good portion of the Board of Directors was in favor of selling and that you had a year to buy out both him and Brigitte. You know the rest."

"So they fired him for not divulging company secrets?" Jack thought that sounded cold, even for Oven Love.

"What it boiled down to is he wasn't providing any value." Laura tried to remain serious, but a quick laugh escaped. "Can you imagine? Hiring Scott to get company secrets?"

"Yeah. That's funny." Jack tried to picture Scott in a big office with drawers full of secret files on Mama Meg's.

"Anyway, he's upset about it. Working for Oven Love was the first job he's gotten on his own. Even though it was with the competition, he was proud of it."

"It made me crazy that he worked there."

"That was one of the other things he loved about working at Oven Love."

Jack groaned.

"So I took advantage of his downtrodden state and asked him the big question."

"What big question?" Certainly she wasn't asking him to come back to Mama Meg's.

"I asked if he'd consider giving us another six months to buy him and Brigitte out."

"You what?"

"You know we're not ready to spend that kind of money, Jack. We're just three months away from our year deadline, and I don't see how it's going to happen. I just thought, since we were celebrating, Scott might see how well things were going. He might see that we're good for it and give us a break."

Jack felt like someone had just thrown him a lifeline. His hopes began to lift higher than they'd been in a long time. Six more months would be perfect. It would give them time to open new sales areas, launch new products . . . it would loosen the screws Scott had tightened down on him back when he tried to engineer the takeover. "Did he go for it?" God, he hoped so.

"He didn't," Laura responded, clearly discouraged. "I'm sorry, Jack."

"Well, you gave it a shot." He felt the weight slowly settle back into his shoulders and neck. The lifeline yanked, once more, just out of his grasp. "We still have three months. I'll talk to Allen. He might have some ideas."

"There's more."

"Don't tell me. He wants more money now? And sooner?" Jack seethed.

"No, actually, it's something about Oven Love. He happened to mention that, about three months ago, they landed a huge account with Burger Shack."

Jack thought of the '50s-style restaurant chain. He grew up eating there and still thought they had the best burgers around. In fact, it was the one "fast food" place that Jack's wife approved of since their focus was local ingredients and sustainability. She loved their seasonal specialties, like sweet potato fries in the fall, and the kids couldn't get enough of the fresh strawberry shortcake in the spring. Burger Shack wasn't huge, but with thirty-nine locations throughout two states, they were definitely a prize account worth winning.

"Burger Shack is launching a healthy alternative kids' meal and contracted with Oven Love to supply the organic cookies."

Another win for the enemy, he thought. Could they ever beat Oven Love? "So, we'll just have to work a little harder to get the next big account, that's all," Jack stated, the muscles in his back and neck twisting just a little bit tighter. "Even if Leslie had gotten that sale, we wouldn't have been ready to deliver on it. She'd warned us we needed to get going on the organic line. It's just been slow getting everything just right." This logic was no balm to his wounded ego. How could Oven Love always be one step ahead?

"Well, that's where there might be some good news," Laura said. "Scott says the results from Oven Love's taste tests have been abysmal."

"He actually used the word 'abysmal'?"

"No, he said the cookies 'taste like armpits.'"

"Leave it to Scott . . ."

"Burger Shack is not happy and Oven Love's R&D is scrambling to come up with new recipes as fast as they can. But even if they stumble on a recipe for a cookie that doesn't taste like B.O., at this point, it's going to take longer for Oven Love to make it than Burger Shack is willing to wait."

"So Oven Love is backing out of the contract?" Emotionally, Jack was starting to wear out. Did he dare let his hopes soar one more time? If Burger Shack was looking for an organic cookie that tasted good, Mama Meg's could definitely deliver.

"They're not backing out, but Burger Shack isn't going to wait. They need a supplier who can give them a good-tasting organic cookie now."

It was one of those moments where Jack knew he and Laura were thinking the exact same thing. "If we can get that contract . . ." he started to say.

"I know," Laura exclaimed, barely able to hold back her excitement.

"Our profits go way up . . ."

"I know!" She actually squealed.

"We can take that to the bank and use it to get a loan to pay off Scott and Brigitte."

"Jack," she said, "this is it. This is how we buy out Scott and Brigitte. This is our miracle!"

"I just can't believe Scott basically dropped this in our lap. Does he even realize how much this is going to help us?"

"He's worked pretty hard cultivating his 'black sheep' status. I don't think he's going to give that up right away, but I'm certain he knew exactly what he was telling us. He knows he's been a pain in your ass. I think this is his way of extending a peace offering."

"Well, it's one hell of a peace offering." If Scott wanted to make it up to him, he had a long way to go. One good deed couldn't erase years of bad behavior. Although, this was a spectacularly good deed.

"Jack?" Laura asked. "When are you going to let Leslie know?"

"I just hit 'send' on the text. I expect she'll be calling any second now."

10

Victorious in Battle

"Congratulate me, Jack!" Leslie exclaimed as she strode into his office. "Burger Shack is as good as ours."

It had been just two weeks since Jack had learned about the huge opportunity and it sounded like Leslie had pulled off the sale. "You did it?" Jack beamed, still hesitant to believe his long nightmare with his siblings was about to be over.

"Don't sound so surprised," she responded, her big smile giving away her own sense of giddy amazement. "I told you not to doubt me." She pushed the chair away from the desk with her foot and sat down, stretching her legs out in front of her and throwing her hands behind her head, her elbows sticking out like wings of victory. "I need to celebrate. What've you got back there?" she asked, pointing to the credenza behind his desk. "You must have a bottle of single-malt. Am I right?"

Jack eyed her with a touch of suspicion. Did she have x-ray vision? Without breaking eye contact, he reached back, opened the cupboard, and pulled out a bottle of Glenlivet and two glasses and set them on the desk in front of him.

"Ooh, fifteen-year-old! That will do." She sat up and leaned into the desk eagerly. "You pour and I'll talk."

Jack obeyed.

"I met with Leo and his team this morning and knocked the presentation out of the park. We had enough Mama Meg's organic cookies in that conference room to feed a small nation and they couldn't stop eating them—couldn't believe they were healthy!"

"And they gave us the contract?" Jack asked.

"One thing at a time, Jack," Leslie said, holding out her glass while amber liquid splashed into it.

Jack smiled through his mounting impatience. "Go on, then."

"They're going to let us do a limited roll-out. The healthier version of the kids' meals, with our cookies, will appear in fifteen stores. They'll evaluate after two months, and if things go well, we'll be in all thirty-nine. We're charging more than Oven Love, but they agreed to the price anyway. Burger Shack is desperate since the launch date for the new meal is right around the corner. They've got the advertising in place and the compostable lunch sacks with seeds embedded in the paper have been printed, boxed and ready to ship. It would have been stupid of me not to take advantage of their urgency."

"Of course. Wait . . . how did you know what Oven Love was charging? Did they tell you?"

"I have my ways." Her eyebrows did a little conspiratorial dance.

"You better not have done anything illegal. If Oven Love turns around and sues us after we've gotten this far . . ."

"Jack, it was nothing like that. One of my sales people happened to run into one of Oven Love's sales people at The Salty Dawg and they talked shop over a couple beers. The guy from Oven Love happened to have more than a couple and our guy kept his head. That's all." She shook her head and rolled her eyes like a teenager disgusted with her father. "Frankly, I'm getting a little tired of you always assuming the worst of me. I've done nothing but work my ass off for this company." She set her drink down with a hard smack on the desk as if to punctuate what she was saying. A little whiskey splashed out, but Leslie didn't notice or didn't care. "Your mother liked me. Why don't you? She always said she saw a bit of her younger self in me. She praised me for my creative thinking as a way to stay competitive. I respected the hell out of your mother, Jack. And she respected me. I would never do anything to betray that respect, even though she's gone."

Jack grabbed the bottle, poured some more into his glass, and took a drink, taking his time while he gathered his thoughts. Finally, he spoke, "I'm sorry." He looked up at the walls covered in posters of his mother—posters he'd planned on taking down just a few weeks ago. Margaret had always looked for a different way to do things; a creative angle to be worked that others had overlooked. That was one of the things that made her so successful. She'd donated hundreds of thousands of cookies to elementary schools on the hunch that the kids would eat her cookies for lunch during the week and ask their parents to buy them on the weekend. Her partnership with a local ice cream maker evolved into the wildly popular "Do It Yourself Ice Cream Sandwich Kit" with a coupon for ice cream on every box of Mama Meg's cookies. And, in a move Roald Dahl himself would have championed, she ran a contest for a Cookie Factory experience where kids and their parents could win a tour, help develop a new cookie flavor, be photographed for a new ad campaign and get showered with Mama Meg's gifts, including a year's worth of cookies. That promotion alone was responsible for doubling sales in one year.

Leslie was using the same creative strategies with her Sales department. Why did Jack have such a hard time accepting that? She'd just gotten them in the door with Burger Shack. It was her insistence they get going on the organic cookie line ten months ago that allowed them to be in perfect position to take the business away from Oven Love now. If this deal with Burger Shack truly was the thing that would save Mama Meg's—and it was—and Leslie was the one who made sure they were perfectly positioned to get this deal with Burger Shack . . . was Leslie the one who was saving Mama Meg's?

"Well, good. You should be sorry." Her tone had switched from accusing back to blithe in an instant and Jack wondered if he should put the whiskey away. "Where was I? Oh right! The limited roll-out." She picked up her drink again and leaned back in the chair, one arm across her stomach while the other, holding the glass, gestured along with the story. "We're as good as in, Jack. There's no way our cookie won't win over everyone who tastes it."

"How do you know?"

"Well, have you tasted it? It's fantastic!" Leslie's hand flew into the air as a way to make her point and Jack watched as her drink slopped up the edges of the highball, barely keeping to its glassy confines.

"I have tasted it. And it's great. But how can you be so confident?"

"Well, a few months back, I got my hands on one of Oven Love's armpit cookies. I turned it over to R&D so they knew exactly what we were up against. That sped up the development of our cookie, of course."

Jack resisted his initial urge to accuse Leslie of corporate espionage again and instead, took a calming breath and said, "How in the world did you get Oven Love's cookie?"

"It was Soren," she replied, as if it were obvious.

"Soren Ackerman gave you a top secret, still-in-development cookie?" Jack knew there was more to the story. "Have they fired him yet?"

Leslie laughed. "He doesn't know he gave it to me. And I'm not going to tell. And besides," she chuckled to herself, "he didn't exactly place it in my hand."

"Go on."

"Remember how you overheard me talking on the phone about Soren and thought I might be giving *him* company secrets?"

Jack nodded slowly but deliberately. How could he forget?

"I won't lie. It hurt that you doubted me. At the time I wasn't sure anything would come of my little fishing expedition and didn't want to worry you. I knew you'd overreact if you knew what I was doing."

Jack attempted to protest but Leslie wouldn't let him.

"You've been behind the desk too long, Jack. You have to know this kind of thing happens a lot. Marcia hires competitive intelligence researchers all the time. It's a huge part of her marketing strategy to know what the competition is doing. She has to know what she's up against. We all do."

Of course this made sense, but at the same time, it surprised him. The thought of employing spies seemed underhanded. "So, you were trying to get secrets out of Soren?" he demanded, trying to nudge her back to the story before he thought too long and hard about the spying.

"I got wind that Oven Love was onto something big. I didn't know what it was, but I knew Soren would have a hard time not gloating about it to me, given our history . . ."

She trailed off, leaving Jack to fill in blanks he didn't want to fill in.

"Anyway," she said, getting back to the story, "he was pretty much a vault. I couldn't get a lick of information out of him. But I didn't give up. Over a few weeks of going out for drinks and talking, I told him stuff he already knew; about how the Board was starting to lean towards selling to Oven Love, the issues with your brother and sister—stuff like that—thinking that I could let him think I might be looking for a job. Maybe if he thought I was on his side he would let something slip. But it turns out, Soren knows me well, too. I think he saw right through the whole ruse. But he did throw me one crumb, so to speak." Her eyes lit up as she recalled the story.

Jack was riveted and finding himself impatient. "The cookie?" he guessed.

"Not quite. But he mentioned 'organic.'"

Jack thought back to all those meetings in which Leslie had essentially demanded a new line of organic cookie. In the middle of his biggest financial challenge, she'd been pushing for new products. It hadn't made a lot of sense at the time. But now . . . "Why didn't you just tell me Oven Love was making an organic line of cookies? I'm sure I would have been more supportive. Everyone would have."

"I needed to play this close to the vest and see how it evolved. I didn't want to give away too much at first in case my suspicions were off."

"So then, how'd you get the cookie?"

"Oh, that's easy. I signed up for the focus group." Leslie folded her arms and leaned back in her chair, a satisfied smile stretching across her face.

"*You* went to an Oven Love focus group for that armpit cookie? You. The VP of Sales for Mama Meg's Cookies walked right in the front doors of our biggest competitor. . ."

"It was actually at some downtown marketing research company."

"And no one recognized you?"

"Nope." She leaned forward to grab her whiskey, then resumed her smug posture and took a drink.

"Don't they choose people randomly for those things? I don't get it. How in the world..."

"I've known what firm Oven Love uses to run their focus groups, thanks to Marcia's competitive intelligence agents," she said, emphasizing the last two words and looking pointedly at Jack. "I signed up to get on their list and got an invitation to take part. I would go when I thought it would be relevant and skip the rest. But when I got an invite to give feedback on an 'organic baked treat,' I had a feeling I'd hooked something big."

"They don't give away the name of the company behind the product at those things. How did you know?"

"It was a lucky guess. Also, I snapped a few pictures of the company reps that were there for the focus group and had Marcia check it out with one of her guys."

"Spying, again?"

"It's called *corporate information gathering*, and it's perfectly legal. One hundred percent above board, Jack."

"Of course. I didn't mean to imply . . ."

"Relax." Leslie took the last swallow of whiskey and set her glass on the desk in front of her. "I know I've been a pain in your ass these last few months." She looked down into her lap briefly, then back up, looking Jack right in the eyes. "And truth be told, I'll probably continue to be a pain in the ass. You don't have to worry about me, though. I might walk the edge of what is morally and legally right, but I won't cross it. If people want to give me helpful information, I'm going to use it."

"I think that's what my mom liked so much about you. You have a lot in common with her. I don't know why I didn't see it before."

"Stop!" she said with feigned modesty.

"No, I mean it, Leslie. Thank you. For all you have done, thank you. Because of this deal, I think the bank will give me the money to buy out Scott and Brigitte. I'm finally going to get them off my back, we can move forward with confidence from the Board, we keep this a family company. It sounds like I owe a lot of those things to you."

For once, Leslie seemed to be at a loss for words. She cocked her head to the side and looked at Jack like she was seeing him for the first time. She smiled and after what seemed like a minute or two, said, "You are most welcome." She pushed back her chair and stood. "I guess I'd better get back to work. I've got to update my sales plan. I'm looking for other regional fast food outlets in our new territories. I'm going to put a promo piece together that highlights our work with Burger Shack and send my sales people out."

"That sounds like a lot of work."

"Not really; I can automatically update the CRM and it will go out to all the sales people."

"That's fantastic. I keep having to remind myself that we don't have to do things the hard way anymore. It feels great."

Leslie moved for the door, opened it and stepped halfway out of Jack's office, then turned back and declared, "Just remember: don't ever underestimate me in a competition against Soren Ackerman."

* * *

The production floor was humming with activity, while the percussion of packaging machines kept a steady beat that reverberated throughout the whole facility. Jack had to shout so Chris could hear him as they walked past a giant oven baking chocolate chip cookies. The smells of warm butter, chocolate and sugar drifted into Jack's nostrils like Sirens of smell attempting to lure him away. Only years of being around that smell allowed him to stay focused now. "How are things looking for our Burger Shack order? Are we going to be ready? We're definitely going to need to give this one priority."

"No need to shove other orders out of the way," Chris shouted, then said something Jack couldn't quite make out.

"What?" Jack cupped his ear and turned his head to hear better. They'd finally reached Chris's office and Chris held the door while Jack stepped in.

"I've got a much clearer picture of the supply chain and how sales projections will affect it," Chris stated, closing the door behind them. "I have a pretty good idea of what's coming down the line six months from now. I'm not putting out fires all the time. I can get in front of problems and it's much easier to plan."

"That's what I like to hear," Jack responded, taking a seat across from Chris.

Chris rubbed the back of his neck and shook his head. "It's exciting to see. I have to play it cool in front of these young guys on the line so they don't think I'm some relic. They're used to technology working like this."

"What do you mean?"

"I just can't believe how smooth this all works. When Sales puts in an order, the recipe gets automatically configured in our system. It looks at inventory and sees if we have enough ingredients. If we don't, it orders what we need. It's seamless."

"That does sound impressive."

"That's not all." Chris pushed back from his desk and sent his chair rolling over to his computer. He typed a few characters and opened up a page. "Check this out. Here's a list of orders that are scheduled to ship today. I can see where they are in the process and as soon as they go out the door, an invoice goes out to the customer. Just like that."

Chris was like a kid on Christmas morning, showing off his newest toy. Jack smiled to himself.

"See this customer here?" Chris pointed at the screen. "They're a long-time customer we've had a relationship with for years. We've got it set up that their invoices are automatically paid through their bank."

"No kidding." Jack leaned forward to get a better look.

"And, I've been able to work out a deal with some of our suppliers so they can have access to our ERP system. When inventories reach a certain point, we've got auto ship set up so new supplies get sent right away. It's a beautiful thing, Jack." Chris leaned back in his chair, a satisfied look on his face.

"You've got more time to be proactive instead of reactive," Jack said.

"Ha, ha! Leave it to the boss to put it like a business self-help book. I don't care what kind of label you put on it. I've got my day back, that's all I know."

Jack nodded, accepting the jab. "This is great news. So we're going to be good for Burger Shack?" Jack brushed at the fine dusting of flour coating the sleeve of his shirt.

"Burger Shack is going to be a challenge. We're not ready for it today, but I'm confident we'll be up to speed in time. We will be able to run their product for a while, but if projections hold, and if this is as big as we think, we won't have the production facility to keep up."

"We're not in a position to acquire another facility right now. How long do you think we have?"

"If we bring in another shift, we should be okay for a while, maybe a year. But that means pay differentials for the night shift workers; it's more money."

"That's true, but it will keep us going for a while." Jack wondered how long they would keep going, then realized he could look at the cost of keeping that third shift compared to the cost of a new facility with reports Walt could run on the new ERP system. He could know exactly the right time to buy a new facility. He relaxed some at the thought. Maybe it made more sense to start looking for a new facility now?

"We can also look at product profitability," Chris added. "Maybe we could cut one or more of the cookie varieties—our lowest-sellers, maybe? That could free up a lot of resources for the expanded operations."

"That shouldn't be too difficult to figure out. Walt should be able to help us with that. We can bring it up at the next meeting and get input as well."

Muffled thumping and humming seeped through the walls along with the ever-present scent of cookies. Jack's stomach grumbled. Maybe he wasn't as immune to the lure of warm cookies as he thought.

"We wouldn't have been able to handle Burger Shack's order a year ago. You know that, right?" Chris said.

"Yeah. Things were a lot less efficient back then. Seems like so long ago."

"It's not just increased efficiency. I can make projections now like I never could before. The ERP upgrade means I can trust the numbers I'm getting. And it's been a godsend to have the sales numbers linked into my system. The decisions I'm making now? They're solid. No more guessing. I can say with certainty that we will be ready for Burger Shack."

* * *

Walt stood and paced the length of his office as Jack laid out his plan.

"We stand to grow this company by thirty percent within a year. That's how big Burger Shack is for us. When it takes off—and it will—we will get a huge bump in sales. We're going to need to ramp up productions, bring on another shift, and purchase new raw materials and packaging. There will be advertising costs and promotion as well."

"I agree," Walt said, still pacing. "It makes sense to get a loan for the operating costs. But buying out your brother and sister? That's a huge financial risk, Jack. Do we really want to put ourselves under that much pressure? If there's any kind of downturn . . . if anything happens . . . they can call the loan. It would crush us."

"I don't have a choice, Walt." Jack understood Walt's concern about taking a big loan from the bank, but surely he had to realize it came down to keeping or losing the company. If he lost the company, this order from Burger Shack and all the capital they needed to deliver the product would be irrelevant. They had to buy out Scott and Brigitte and they had to do it now. There was a little over five weeks until his year was up. Barely enough time to work out the loan details with the bank.

"Maybe Oven Love won't be in a position to buy. They just lost this huge hamburger deal, after all. Maybe they don't have the capital to do it. Did you ever think of that?" Walt asked, his cheeks flush with some emotion that seemed to be bubbling just below the surface. "If there's no buyer, there's no sale."

"I'm sure Scott can find another buyer." Jack hoped Scott would never go to those lengths to destroy Mama Meg's. He felt like recently he'd seen a glimpse of humanity in his brother. But he couldn't be sure. The money he'd get from the sale was a very big motivation for him.

"And the Board!" Walt said, shooting his finger into the air while his eyes lit up with sudden inspiration. "The Board will surely be on your side now. Like you stated, Burger Shack represents a thirty percent growth over the next year. They can't ignore that. They'd be idiots! There's no way your brother would have anyone standing with him now in favor of the sale." Walt's pacing had stopped and he stood directly in front of Jack, making his case with a surprising amount of passion.

"We've got a contract, Walt. Remember? I signed it, Scott signed it, John Linde witnessed and notarized it. It's legally binding. I'm buying out Scott and Brigitte and I'm going to be done with them."

If there had been a light in Walt's eyes before, at Jack's words, it went out. Walt seemed to actually deflate as he lowered himself into a chair in resignation. "I just wish there was some way to get around them. It makes me sick to think of that much money going out the door with nothing to show for it."

"I know it's your job to keep Mama Meg's financially stable. And you have always done a great job at that, Walt. It's probably as natural as breathing for you to question every dollar we spend. I'm sure it's hard to watch us spend that kind of money . . . to be in debt to the bank that much. It makes me a little sick to my stomach, too." Jack gave a nervous laugh.

"You have no idea," Walt responded.

"But I'm confident that this Burger Shack deal is just the start of greater things for us, Walt. We are perfectly poised for continued growth over the next few years. While the huge loan does make me a little uneasy, the thought of where we will be in five years thrills me and I have to move forward with confidence. Don't worry." He smiled with what he hoped was assurance. "Everything is going to be fine."

"I pray you're right." Walt's face had blanched and Jack thought he saw a tinge of green.

"Honestly, Walt!" Jack said, giving him a couple good-natured claps on the back. "It's going to be okay. Don't you trust me?"

"Trust?" Walt shook his head and laughed, looked up at Jack and smiled. "I trust you, Jack. Of course I do."

11

An Attack from the Inside

It was a tight fit getting all four of them into John Linde's office. Jack always wondered why John's office hadn't grown at the same rate his status at the law firm had. Looking around at the plaque-covered walls, the shelves lined with hundreds of matching law books, piles of paperwork stacked up on almost every surface, and a collection of vintage and historic gavels tucked into corners and perched on the corner of his desk, Jack figured it was probably easier to stay where he was than to move the whole menagerie to a well-deserved corner office.

The warm, woodsy scent of the leather couch did little to soothe the bitter feelings that thickened the atmosphere in the room. Jack sat on the edge, knowing if he relaxed back into the soft cushions, he would lose his air of sharp authority he was attempting to maintain. A checklist of Scott's offenses played on a loop in his mind; all reasons he didn't deserve this huge windfall and shouldn't have been able to wield so much power over his and Laura's lives for the last year.

Scott looked smug and unlike Jack—at ease as he sat, legs extended, in the club chair shoved into the corner of John's office. Or was it all a show? A smoke screen of calm to cover a storm of moral conflict inside? Jack laughed to himself at the thought. *Scott and moral conflict?* There's two things he never thought he'd hear in the same sentence.

Laura was seated next to Jack on the couch in a slightly less defensive position. She'd drilled Jack with dos and don'ts on the ride over: Do give Scott and Brigitte the benefit of the doubt; Don't take it personally; Do be on your best behavior; Don't yell; Do be civil and just get this the hell over with.

Brigitte was seated on a padded folding chair they'd pulled in from another room. She had her Gucci bag on her lap and was texting on her phone, oblivious to the tension in the room. She laughed out loud at something she read, then looked up, as if suddenly remembering where she was, cleared her throat and slid her phone into her purse. "Sorry," she said with an apologetic grin.

"Well, are we all ready to begin?" John said.

It was a rhetorical question, but Scott sat up and declared, "I am," then looked at Jack and Laura as if they would answer, too.

Jack seethed and took a slow, deep breath. That was also something Laura had told him to do. "It will help you relax, Jack. In for ten, out for ten. Count slowly." She'd made him practice in the car.

"Yes," Laura smiled. "I'm ready, too. Let's do this."

She was clearly trying to relieve some of the pressure in the room. But why? For Scott? He didn't deserve to have this go easily. Jack counted slower. In . . . out.

"All I need is a few signatures," John said, spreading a stack of paperwork out on limited real estate that was his desktop. Brightly colored sticky tabs with arrows pointed to the place where Jack would gift his brother with more money than he could ever need, but that he would surely find a way to use. In . . . out.

Brigitte was the first to lean in and sign. She finished with a flourish and asked, "What's the date?" John turned his desk calendar towards her and she finished and slid the pen towards Jack and Laura.

When he hesitated, Laura grabbed it and quickly added her signature, leaving the pen on the desk instead of handing it off to Jack.

Scott stood and approached to sign next. He leaned over the desk, his butt coming within inches of Jack's face.

Jack tensed and slid back into the couch to put some space between him and Scott's ass. *To hell with slow breathing*, he thought, and began to tighten his jaw. If this wasn't a metaphor for the whole last year, he didn't know what was. It was as if Scott had been saying, "I'm going to do whatever I want, and you can just kiss my ass."

Jack's jaw tightened more. *How dare he! That selfish little . . .*

Jack felt the slightest pressure on his forearm and looked down to see Laura's hand resting there. He looked at her and she smiled, then widened her eyes as if to silently convey an important message; to jog Jack's memory of something important.

"Wait, was I supposed to sign with my middle initial?" Scott asked. "It says Scott J. McCallister, but I only signed 'Scott McCallister.' That's cool, right?"

While John answered Scott's question, Jack gave Laura a puzzled look and her eyes widened and her smile grew. And then he remembered.

"Above all," Laura had said on the car ride over, "do remember that by signing, it's not Scott that wins. It's us."

Jack hadn't followed her logic at first, but she explained.

"Sure, Scott is going to get an obscene amount of money, but once we sign, it's over."

Jack thought about it.

"It's over," Laura repeated. "He has no more say in the company. No more sway with the Board. No claim on anything. He's out. Your signing those documents marks an end to his destructive presence and the beginning to us moving forward with the goal to grow Mama Meg's into a national brand. We win."

Laura still had that big smile plastered across her face, as if it actually had the power to shoot out calming vibes. As John pointed out several other places for Scott to sign, Jack felt his jaw loosen and his body relax. He actually let himself sink back into the couch and let the soft leather comfort him. This was going to be okay.

Laura gave a self-satisfied smirk and probably went on to silently contemplate her potential super power: breaking tension with a single glance!

"Oh, dude!" Scott exclaimed, turning to face Jack. "My ass was totally in your face." He seemed genuinely surprised and uncharacteristically embarrassed at the discovery. "Sorry, brother." He put his hand on Jack's shoulder and looked him in the eye, searching for something. Waiting for whatever reply Jack might have to give.

For the first time that morning, Jack felt at peace with the situation. Maybe Laura did have super powers after all. "It's all good, Scott. All forgiven."

Scott looked at Jack for a moment, waiting for some caveat or exception, but there was none. A huge smile broke across his face.

"Here," Jack said, extending his hand. "Help me up. I think John's couch is trying to eat me alive."

Scott grasped Jack's hand and pulled him to standing.

"Now, where's that pen?"

* * *

Laura had been right. Being out from under the intense and constant threat of losing Mama Meg's did wonders for Jack's mood. In the weeks after, he'd called Allen and filled him in on the good news: Burger Shack, paying off Scott and Brigitte, and opportunities for expansion. Allen had been finishing up business in Santiago, but made plans to sit down and talk with Jack when he got back the next week.

He'd met with Tom earlier in the week, who had agreed that Gordon was coming along well and would probably be ready to step in as CIO in the next six months. Leslie was making inroads in the new sales regions and had a couple very solid leads with regional fast food restaurants who were interested in developing a healthy kids' meal similar to Burger Shack's.

"My sales people can see exactly what's in inventory and know for a fact when things will ship," Leslie had gushed to him a few days ago. "Do you know what kind of advantage that gives us in closing sales? I don't think we'd be doing half as well in our new territories if we were still doing things the old way." It was hard not to agree. "And we're able to attract bigger customers, too; customers who are used to that level of service from their sales people."

"What is the timeline for expansion?" Jack asked Laura over lunch one afternoon.

"We were looking at a new facility a few miles from here that would need just a few modifications to get up and running. We wanted to be ready in a couple months. But everything is on hold now until the audit is over," she said.

"Audit?"

"Walt didn't tell you?"

"I don't think I've talked to Walt for a couple days. What's up?"

"Just a routine audit from the bank. They'll be working on it for the next week."

"You don't think this is because of the huge line of credit we just took out . . . to pay off Scott and Brigitte and for the expansion? It seems a little soon. Do you think I should be worried? What did Walt say?"

"Walt didn't tell me about it. I heard about it from Marcia, who was trying to get in touch with someone in Finance with questions about her budget. Things are a little crazy over there while they pull everything the bank wants to look at. But it is definitely routine."

"I guess you're right," Jack replied. "So, do you have any idea when we'll be able to move forward with the expansion? I'd hate to wait too long and run into trouble getting Burger Shack's product out the door."

"You'd better check with Walt on that," Laura answered, shoving the last few bites of Cobb salad into her mouth. "I've got a meeting with Chris, so I've got to get out of here." She stood up to leave, grabbed her garbage and then said, "Let me know what you hear from Walt, though, will you?"

"I will." Jack finished his lunch and thought about how things would change when they added another facility. This never could have happened without the upgrade to their ERP system and the training everyone went through to become proficient. Things were running so smoothly now and information was so easily available, making decisions about how to move forward could be done with confidence and assurance.

Jack and Chris had looked at production numbers and determined how long they could run product through their current facility before hitting critical mass. It wasn't a guess or a hunch. It was an exact number of weeks. Because of this specific data, they could be ready; not too soon and not too late, but at the best time production-wise and finance-wise.

He thought back to the conversation he'd had with Allen almost a year ago and how hesitant he'd been to bring Emmett in to help. It was laughable to think about in hindsight, knowing how well everything had turned out.

Of all the people Jack could have as a mentor and friend, he was glad it was Allen.

* * *

Jack knew Walt would be busy, so he decided to walk down to his office and see if he could catch him instead of trying to call. "Hi, Jonathan," he said to the personal assistant sitting at the front desk. "I'm just going to pop in and ask Walt a quick question."

"He said he had some appointments and would be out all afternoon. Do you want me to let him know you stopped by?"

Before he could answer, he heard a familiar voice from behind him.

"Jack." He turned around to see Gordon carrying a folded up laptop under his arm. "Do you have a few minutes?"

He said he did and they found an empty office and sat down.

"As you know, I was involved with setting up and training on the Fixed Assets module that went into our ERP upgrade," Gordon started. "I've been overseeing the transfer of all the spreadsheets into the system."

"It sounds like a big job." Jack wasn't sure where Gordon was going with this.

"It is. It is. But that's not what I want to talk about. One of our guys who was helping with the transfer noticed something that didn't seem right on one of the spreadsheets. I've been looking at it and I think we might have a problem."

"What do you mean? What kind of problem?"

"I'm not sure, but the numbers are way off. It's way too big to just be a math error." Gordon shifted in his seat. "I talked to Tom about it and he agreed something wasn't right. He advised me to bring it to Walt . . . see if he could explain it. But Walt's not here."

"Okay, well, after Walt and his department have had time to pull everything the auditors want, we can have Walt take a look at it. I'm sure we can figure it out. Just put it aside until he's back."

"It can't wait, Jack. This is one of the balance sheets the auditors are asking for. I'm an IT guy, not a finance guy, but even I can tell something's not right."

"When do they need it?" Jack felt a twinge in his gut, but pushed it aside.

"By the end of today."

"See if you can hold them off until tomorrow morning. We will get Walt to look at it first thing."

"And if I can't hold them off?"

"Then hand it over. We can always follow up with them later when we get more information."

* * *

"I'm glad Gordon caught that," Walt said over the phone the next morning. "As soon as I get in I'll have a chat with the head auditor and get that all straightened out."

"Thanks, Walt. I knew there had to be a simple explanation." Jack felt tension he didn't even know he'd been carrying slip off his shoulders.

"No problem, but just for the record, this is one of the things I knew would be a problem when we switched from spreadsheets to the Fixed Asset program." He chuckled out loud to make sure Jack knew he was making a joke. Walt's days of protesting the expensive ERP upgrade were well behind him.

"Well, when you fix it, it will have been a minor inconvenience in the overall success of the project, wouldn't you say?"

"It will be lost in the noise, I'm sure," Walt replied.

"We'll see you when you get in, then."

"Sounds good," Walt said before signing off.

Nothing to worry about, Jack said to himself. *I knew it would be nothing to worry about.*

* * *

It was easy to get caught up in the changes that were happening at Mama Meg's. The new acquisition was back on track now that the audit was mostly done. In the week that the bank auditors had been on-site, locked in the conference room and keeping the Finance department hopping with their requests for information, Jack had been on a site visit to the proposed new facility and spent more time looking over potential equipment to purchase with Chris. Things were moving along.

Once they got past the audit, they would be free to move forward.

Jack's phone buzzed with a call from his assistant. "Mr. Clayton, from the bank, would like to see you for a few minutes. The auditors have just wrapped up and are getting ready to leave."

"Send him in," Jack answered, quickly clearing off a space on his desk that had become cluttered with a week of ignored mail and messages.

"Mr. McCallister, thanks for seeing me. I just wanted to check in with you before we leave." He looked exactly what you'd expect a bank auditor to look like: wiry frame, thick glasses, and deathly serious. He probably wouldn't know a joke if it came up and bit him on the butt. He sat tentatively on the edge of the chair across from Jack's desk, as if he didn't plan on staying long.

"We've finished up with the audit and will be compiling our report. We should have that ready by the end of the week."

"Great," Jack said. "We're eager to hear the findings and move forward with our expansion."

"Well, I wanted to let you know," Mr. Clayton cleared his throat as if the words were getting stuck, "we found some significant discrepancies on the balance sheets."

"What do you mean?" Jack asked. "What do you mean by, 'significant'?"

"We realize there have been some bumps in the road as you've switched over from the spreadsheets to using the ERP's Fixed Assets module. It's a good module and very accurate—nearly impossible to hide actual numbers."

"Why would anything have been hidden?" Jack couldn't keep the rising panic out of his voice.

"It's common for things like this," Mr. Clayton coughed lightly to indicate he was choosing his words carefully, "to surface when you switch from a manually maintained system, like your spreadsheets, to one that is automatically maintained."

"You talked to Walt, though, right? One of the balance sheets did have some issues, but Walt said there was an explanation. He talked to you about that, right?" Jack still wasn't entirely sure what was happening.

"Walt has not contacted us. His personal assistant says he hasn't been in all week."

* * *

Jack spent the rest of the afternoon leaving messages on Walt's voice mail in between several long discussions with Laura, phone calls to John Linde, and meeting with his executive team.

"Walt maintained the spreadsheets," Laura kept repeating. "He was the one who had full control over them."

Jack tried to remember the last time he'd spoken with him and how he'd just assumed Walt was on his way into work. How had he not noticed that he'd been missing all week? "Did anyone else notice he hadn't been coming in?"

"I noticed," Gordon interjected, "but I assumed you knew. No one in Finance seemed alarmed he wasn't there."

"We've all been so busy," Leslie pointed out. "I've been on a three-day sales trip, you and Chris have been trying to get the expansion plans underway, Marcia has been swamped with developing a new marketing plan for the organic line. I think we all just assumed Walt was busy with the audit."

Everyone nodded thoughtfully.

"Maybe I should try and call him again," Jack said. "I need to know how big this is going to be. I don't want to be blindsided. All the auditor would say was that it was significant."

No one wanted to say what everyone was thinking, but Jack knew they were all aware that if it was big enough of a discrepancy—if Walt had been hiding money or misrepresenting Mama Meg's financial health—it could ruin everything. Scott and Brigitte would be a walk in the park compared to what would happen.

"Call him again," Laura said. "Maybe he'll pick up this time."

"He probably just has his phone off," Leslie asserted. "That's what I'd do if I was trying to avoid facing some idiotic thing I'd done."

"We don't know that Walt's done anything wrong. We don't know exactly why he hasn't been into work for a week," Jack pointed out.

"Yeah, but it sure looks suspicious," Tom countered. "Have we tried to contact his wife?"

"Norma's not picking up either," Jack replied. He picked up his phone, stared at it for a few seconds, wondering if he should even waste his time, then dialed Walt's number again. Everyone seemed to hold their breath, waiting, wondering if this time would be the time Walt answered.

"Voice mail," Jack said and everyone exhaled. It was the most dejected breath of air Jack had ever heard expelled. As for him, the pit in his stomach plumbed new depths as he waited for the beep. "Walt," he said to the voice mail. "It's Jack. Again. Listen, we really need to talk to you. We've got a situation here and we need your help. It's urgent. So please call me back." Jack started to press "end call" but then added one more thing. "And Walt? If you are worried about anything, if you are not answering the phone because you are concerned about us finding out something, please, don't worry. I just want to talk to you." This time, his finger connected with the little red phone icon and the call ended.

He looked around the table. Several people had their heads down, staring at their laps. Chris was shaking his head, staring off into the corner of the room. Laura sat, stone-faced and rigid— her refusal to let any emotion flash across her face or seep out through a clenched fist revealed nothing and everything at the same time.

"Let's call it a day," Jack said with a sigh. "If any of you hear anything, don't hesitate to call me—no matter what time it is." Everyone got up and filed out except for Laura.

After they were gone, Jack wanted to reach out, to touch her arm or her shoulder, to reassure and comfort her, but he found he couldn't even lift his hand to make the empty gesture. He just didn't have it in him.

* * *

The next day, the bank called to say it was putting a hold on Mama Meg's line of credit pending the auditor's report. Walt still hadn't called in. John Linde had laid out several different scenarios based on different outcomes, but none of them were very promising. At an utter loss for what to do, Jack reached out to Allen, but even he was not answering his phone.

"I think we should call the cops," Leslie declared, suddenly appearing in Jack's office like she'd materialized right in front of him.

Jack found it terribly disorienting. "Where did you come from?" he replied, feeling his senses dull. He was either in shock or had been drinking. And he didn't remember drinking, although that wasn't entirely out of the question. He thought of the bottle in the cabinet behind him.

"Just down the hall," Leslie gestured with her hands impatiently. "Now listen! I really think we need to call the cops. About Walt."

"I don't even know what Walt's done, Leslie. I can't just call the cops on him. You have to have a reason."

"No. Not because he may or may not have misrepresented Mama Meg's finances so thoroughly that we may be out of business by next week . . ."

"Stop," he exclaimed. "I get it."

"We need to call the cops," she continued, "because something might have happened. An accident? You said the last you talked to him you thought he was coming into work? Well, what if that was true, and there was an accident?"

"They would have notified Norma by now. We would know if Walt was killed in a car accident a week ago."

"But we haven't heard from Norma either. What if she was with him in the car?"

"He was bringing his wife to work? That doesn't even make sense."

"No!" Leslie threw her hands up in exasperation. "I don't know. I just think we need to consider that we can't contact him because something bad has happened."

"Something bad *has* happened, Leslie." Jack exhaled loudly and Leslie stayed silent for once.

Finally she spoke, softly, with understanding. "Still, he's been missing for days. No one has heard a thing."

"I know."

"I can do it. I can call in a missing persons report."

"Thanks." Jack rubbed his forehead. It occurred to him that if the press got a hold of the story, they could shine a negative light onto Mama Meg's. He pushed that worry aside, though. Did it even matter anymore?

The phone rang and Jack picked up. Leslie waited, in case there was news.

"This is Jack," he said. And then there was silence as Jack simply listened. Leslie shifted on her feet, then sat down to wait it out. Finally, he said, "I understand," and hung up. He turned back to the cabinet behind him, opened the cupboard and pulled out his bottle of Gold Label and two glasses.

"Who was that?" Leslie's voice was soft, but strong.

Jack said nothing while he poured the amber liquid into his glass, then pushed the bottle and second glass across the table to Leslie.

"Jack?" she asked, ignoring the bottle before her.

"That was the bank," he said in between gulps. "They're calling the loan. We have thirty days to repay." He took a long drink of whiskey, then muttered, "I don't see how we can survive this. I think we might be through."

Leslie took the bottle and began pouring her own drink.

"One of the balance sheets had grossly misrepresented our assets. Buildings, equipment we don't have . . . the value of Mama Meg's was being misrepresented to the bank."

"Why?" she held onto her glass as if it were the one thing keeping her tied to reality, but didn't drink. "Why would Walt do that? What could he possibly gain?"

That was indeed the question, wasn't it? Jack thought.

"I can explain," came a voice from the doorway. Walt stood there, his shirt rumpled and his beard with at least three days of tired, grey growth.

"God damn it! Where the hell have you been?" Jack shouted as Walt took a tentative step into the office.

Leslie jumped up and exclaimed, "Walt! It's good to see you." Her easy, suave manner seemed to fail her and she added, "You two, um, probably need to, uh, talk or something." She angled the chair as if to offer the seat to Walt, then looked at Jack, whose look—a mixture of fury and pain—made her think twice.

"I was just leaving anyway," she blurted out, then sidestepped past Walt and made a quick exit.

Walt stood there in silence and Jack got the impression he was trying to keep himself from walking away a second time. Finally, he asked, "May I?" and gestured to the recently vacated chair. He sat, took a deep breath and started, "Jack, you know I've been with this company since before you were riding a two-wheeled bike."

Jack narrowed his eyes at Walt. If he thought he could play the seniority card, he was sadly mistaken.

"Your mom was a fighter. When she started this company, she didn't let anything get in her way. And believe me, there were plenty of things that got in her way. Do you know how many banks turned her down for business loans simply because she was a woman?" Walt got a distant look in his eyes as if remembering. "Those were different times, Jack."

"Walt. The bank just called in our loan. You have a lot to answer for. You said you were going to explain. Now godammit, explain!"

Walt took a deep breath and continued. "I saw how hard she was working—how others made it more difficult for her to succeed. She had to work twice as hard as a man to get the same job done. It wasn't fair." Walt ran his fingers through his thinning hair. "There was a time she needed money to keep going and I knew, I just knew she wasn't going to get it. The bank wanted her to show more growth than they would have required of a male CEO. If she hadn't gotten the loan, she would have been done. So I massaged the numbers—as they say—to make Mama Meg's look better, and so she would get the loan that they would have given to any male CEO that walked in off the street."

"What did you do?"

"I changed the depreciation schedule for the assets. It was a small adjustment, but it was enough, and she got the much-needed money from the bank."

Jack sat silently, trying to put himself in Young Walt's shoes. What would he have done if presented with the same situation?

"It started out small, but it began to snowball. We had to maintain a certain level of assets to keep our line of credit, so I continued to fudge the numbers. I was going to adjust everything once the company got on sure footing, but there were always rough times surrounding every island of success. Even up to last year, I was trying to find a way to fix it. That's why I was so against the consultants coming in and the ERP upgrade. It all just made it worse. Once you start down that path, Jack, it's hard to make the correction. There was never a good time."

Gratitude warred with betrayal inside of Jack as he listened to Walt's story. He'd had the power to right an unfair situation, to level the playing field for his mother, and he'd done it. But in doing so, he'd jeopardized everything she'd worked for. She would have been furious if she'd ever known that he'd cheated for her.

On the other hand, Walt was right: it hadn't been fair. The deck had been stacked against her success.

Walt pulled a folded-up piece of paper from his pocket, opened it and smoothed it out on his leg. He slid it across the table to Jack, then, pointing to Leslie's untouched whiskey, asked, "Do you mind?" He didn't wait for an answer before taking a long drink, then mumbled, "It's my letter of resignation."

Jack's first instinct was to reject it. Walt had been with Mama Meg's for over thirty years. He'd known him since he'd been a small boy. Walt's intentions had been good. But those intentions were going to bring the whole company down. He knew he had to accept it.

"I'm so sorry, Jack." For the first time, Jack noticed how small and worn out Walt looked. The chair seemed to swallow him right up. Maybe it was due to age, but it seemed he had used every bit of reserve strength to come in and talk with Jack. And pushing that resignation letter across the table had just tapped him out.

"I'm sorry, too," Jack said. He picked the letter up off the desk, but didn't look at it. He wasn't ready to look at it yet.

12

Getting a Grip

"Jack, what's going on?" His wife's voice sounded unusually shrill on the other end of the phone and Jack tried to make sense of it. "You didn't come home last night."

Jack opened his eyes just wide enough to focus on the room. The first thing he saw was his mother's face looming over him. He flinched before realizing it was just one of the posters that had fallen off the wall and was now leaning up against the foot of his office sofa. He slowly sat up on the sofa letting gravity pull his feet to the floor, and knocked the whiskey bottle that tipped over and rolled lazy and lopsided under the couch, where it came to rest. It was all starting to come back to him. Walt's admission, the resignation letter, the abandoning of the glass and going straight for the bottle. And there may have been an extremely one-sided conversation with a giant poster of his mother about how she could have missed Walt's deception.

"Jack? Are you there?"

He pulled the phone away from his ear and held onto his forehead, as it was surely seconds from splitting in two. He adjusted the volume and croaked, "I guess I slept at the office."

"God, Jack! You could have been dead on the side of the road for all I knew. You haven't been answering your phone." She sounded more relieved than angry, but there was no denying she was still angry.

"Walt resigned. He's cooked the books and now the bank is calling our loan."

"I know all that. Laura filled me in when I called her to track you down."

"I'm sorry. I just . . . I don't know what I'm going to do."

"I'm sorry, too, Jack."

The phone vibrated and Jack looked to see who was calling. "I'll be home in a little bit, but Allen's calling and I've got to talk to him about this."

Meredith said a quick goodbye and Jack switched over to Allen's call.

"Jack!" Allen's voice was warm and deep and seemed to reverberate in Jack's chest. "I'm back in town and I understand you've bought out your brother and sister. Congratulations. When can we get together to celebrate?"

"Good news, bad news, Allen." The irony was not lost on Jack: so close to success, but so far. "Scott and Brigitte are off my back, but Walt just dropped a bomb yesterday." He filled Allen in on the events of the last week leading up to Walt's admission in his office the day before. "I don't know what to do," he admitted. "Do I start looking for buyers, or file for bankruptcy? Is there any way for me to get through this, because right now it feels like I'm through."

Jack threw himself back into the couch with enough force to shift it slightly from its moorings on the carpet. The poster of his mother started to topple and then crashed to the floor. Jack flinched, then spoke to Allen, "I don't want to be through. Dammit! Tell me it's not over!"

The other end of the line was silent long enough for Jack to wonder if the call had been dropped. But then Allen spoke slowly and deliberately. "This is terrible news, Jack. I don't know what to tell you."

Jack's heart sank hearing the now-dismal tone in his voice. Over the years, Allen had experienced his own business defeats, but he'd worked through them and always come out on top. Deep down, Jack knew that Allen was his only hope. A guide to get him through what felt like Hell. If he had no advice to offer, there was no hope. Jack truly would be through.

"Let me think about it and get back to you," Allen said thoughtfully, and made plans to meet at the beginning of the next week.

"What should I do until then?" Jack asked. He felt hopeless and pressing forward as if everything was fine seemed futile.

"Business as usual, Jack. Don't slow down now."

Jack ended the call and looked around his office. It was just after eight in the morning and the day shift and office employees were just starting to file in. Cars were flowing into the parking lot and he could hear muffled voices and footsteps in the hallway. How could he go about business as usual knowing that any day could be Mama Meg's last? How could he pretend everything was fine when it was anything but?

There was a quick knock at his door and Laura opened it and poked her head in. "Meredith said you'd be here." She came in, pulled a chair over to the couch and handed him a cup of coffee, which he took greedily, suddenly becoming aware of how much he needed it. Laura leaned down and pulled the whiskey bottle out from under the couch. "Really, Jack?" Her eyes were understanding and without judgment.

Jack shrugged. "It seemed like a good time to drink it."

"What time do you want to meet this morning? I can let everyone know."

"Do they all know Walt's gone?"

"I let the team know last night, after you called me."

"Are you able to get a read on what everyone is thinking?" If they all felt like Jack, it was going to be pretty hard to rally any kind of excitement.

"They're confident you will get us through this, Jack. And so am I."

Jack nodded, but didn't say anything. They would get through this all right, but whether or not they still had Mama Meg's when they came through it was still an unknown.

* * *

Despite Laura's assurances of everyone's faith in his leadership, the conference room was solemn as a funeral that afternoon. Filled with his team, yet unnaturally silent as everyone sat, waiting to hear what he'd say. Leslie didn't even have her phone out, and was giving Jack her full attention, which Jack found most disturbing of all.

"How's everyone doing this afternoon?" He was unsure of how to start and apparently everyone was unsure how to respond because no one replied. He continued, "As you've all heard, Walt has resigned as Chief Financial Officer. Years ago, Walt misrepresented our assets so that Mama Meg's could get a badly-needed loan. This discrepancy stayed on the books and grew year after year until the bank discovered it a few weeks ago. The amount is significant enough that the bank has called in our loan. We have thirty days to repay."

"Do we have any way of coming up with that kind of money in thirty days? Another bank maybe?" Leslie asked. "We still have the business prospects. Things are just about ready to blow up, sales-wise. That's got to count for something."

"I don't know if we can work with another bank, but keep moving forward with those sales, Leslie. In fact," Jacked looked at each person at the table, "everyone, keep going with our long-term goals in mind."

"We're nearly at full production capacity," Chris said. "I don't suppose we will be able to do anything about that new facility?"

"That's on hold for now, Chris. But do what you can to keep up with demand."

"I can help you tweak the SCADA system to give you a little more output," Gordon said to Chris. "We'll make sure we are getting every bit of efficiency from our systems while we're waiting for the expansion."

"Thanks, Gordon. That would be great," Jack said quietly.

"What about finding a replacement for Walt?" Laura queried. "Are we going to start that process?"

"Not now. I'm going to meet with Ajay, the Director of Finance, and talk to him about captaining the ship for a month or two."

"Two months? You think that's how long we have? How long before . . ." Marcia couldn't seem to find the words to finish her sentence.

"Are we going to have to file for bankruptcy?" Laura said, finally voicing what everyone else was probably wondering.

"I don't know." Jack was abrupt, frustrated he didn't have more to offer them. "I've spoken with Allen about it and we're going to talk early next week."

"Did he give you any indication . . ." Laura trailed off.

"All he said was that he didn't know what to tell me, and that he would think about it."

No one said anything and all wore a version of despondency on their faces.

"Listen." Jack brought his open palm down on the table with a smack, getting their attention. "I realize this is pretty bad— maybe as bad as it can get. I don't know what the best course of action is. But I trust Allen. If he says to look for a buyer and cut our losses, I know that will be our best option. If he tells us to file for bankruptcy, that's what we're going to do. He has been a friend and mentor for too many years for me not to trust him now."

Jack rose from his chair and started to pace the room. "But until we talk tomorrow, we need to move forward as if this were just a regular day in a regular week. Not a *regular* day, but our best day." He circled the table. "Sell more cookies, Leslie!" he exclaimed, shooting his finger in her direction. "Keep rolling out that marketing plan, Marcia!" he said with another point of his finger. "Chris! You're going to figure out a way to get as much out of our equipment as possible."

"With Gordon's help, I am!" Chris reached across the table and exchanged fist bumps with Gordon.

"Laura, you make sure Chris has what he needs to fill all of our orders."

The tension that had been in the room was replaced with a feeling of purpose. Chris and Gordon were smiling as they checked each other's calendar availability. Marcia said something to Laura that made her laugh. "What are *you* going to do, Jack?" Leslie asked with a sly grin. She'd leaned back in her chair and her phone was in front of her on the desk. Jack had never been so happy to see that phone.

"I'm going to make sure all of you are doing what you're supposed to. And so help me, if I find that anyone has been posting their résumé online, I will personally take it down myself." Jack hoped they all got his thinly-veiled joke, and when they laughed, he knew they had. "I need every one of you to give me everything you've got. Because the next few weeks will probably be rough, and I need to know you all have my back."

* * *

"Allen is on his way up," Laura said, walking into Jack's office the next Tuesday morning and taking a seat. Allen had suggested both of them be present during their meeting as both of them were majority shareholders in Mama Meg's and their discussion would affect its future. "Did he give you any indication of what he's thinking?" Her voice was cool and in control, but her white-knuckled, knotted hands in her lap betrayed her true feelings.

"Not a thing. I still just see two options: file for bankruptcy, or find a buyer, quick."

"Do you think Mom knew what Walt was doing? She had to have some idea. The bank isn't giving her the time of day and then suddenly she gets a loan? She had to be suspicious."

Jack thought about his mom. She was ambitious and never took "no" for an answer. She worked hard and always found a way to do the impossible. But she was no dummy. Was this just one of her methods of getting her way? Was Walt protecting her memory by only giving half the story and taking the fall? "I don't know." He thought back to the years he'd worked by her side, learning the business from the ground up; starting on the production floor as a teenager and then moving to part-time office jobs as he worked through college. In all the years he'd watched his mother run this business, he could not remember a single time she took a shortcut with her product, with how she treated her employees, or with her morals. Even more than that, all that she'd done was to prepare Jack for this day: the day he'd be running the company and have to make hard decisions. Finally he said, "If she'd known, she would have told me. I know she would have told me."

Laura nodded, content with the answer, when Jack's assistant appeared in the doorway.

"Mr. Paulson is here to see you," she announced, and stepped aside, making room for Allen to step in the office.

"Allen." Jack stood up and reached for his hand. Laura did the same. "It's great to see you. Thanks for meeting with us today." He gestured to the open seat next to Laura.

"How are you holding up?" Allen asked.

"It's been tough. We had success in our grasp: Burger Shack and the expansion—it was huge. Everyone was excited. And now this . . ."

"The executive team is moving forward, trying to stay positive, but the possibilities are definitely in the back of their minds," Laura articulated.

"Whatever happens," Jack declared, "we'll get through it." He smiled and shrugged. "What other choice do we have, but to get through it?"

"I know you will," Allen agreed. "Over the last year, you've shown great leadership. The way you've turned things around has been impressive."

"Your advice to bring in Emmett and Tom was key in making that happen."

"Take the compliment, Jack. You and your team had to do the work. What I'm seeing here is that you've turned Mama Meg's from a sputtering, unreliable, old jalopy to a well-oiled machine that has been finely tuned and primed for maximum efficiency. You've got quality products with a huge demand for organics. The market is wide open, and you are perfectly positioned to capitalize on that."

"Which is what makes this current situation all the more hard to swallow."

"Well, I have a solution for that. I like what I've been seeing, Jack. I like it a lot. So much so that I am willing to come in as a major investor." Allen let that sentence hang as if it explained everything, but Jack was not sure what he was getting at.

Jack pushed a piece of paper with the bank's letterhead across the desk so Allen could see it. "This is how much we owe the bank, Allen. I'm not sure we're that good of a bet right now."

"I'm not just looking for a few shares of Mama Meg's." He tapped the paper and pushed it back across the table towards

Jack, as if it meant nothing. "I can take care of what you owe the bank and finance the purchase of the new facility until you work out another line of credit."

Jack looked at Laura, unsure that he was hearing things correctly. Her mouth was hanging open and she appeared to be trying to process the information.

"So you . . ." Laura started. "We just . . ." She looked at Jack for help.

"What exactly are you proposing?" Jack was still trying to process why Allen hadn't said the words "bankruptcy" or "buyer" yet. Was it possible there was a third option he hadn't considered?

"If I'm not mistaken, with your buyout of Scott and Brigitte, you and Laura each now own thirty-five percent of the Mama Meg's stock, for a combined seventy percent controlling interest."

"Yes, that's correct." Laura's voice brightened as if a light had just gone off in her head. Jack was starting to catch up, too.

"I'll take nineteen percent of that stock, which will leave you both with fifty-one percent, combined. I don't want to be involved in the operation. I just want to be an investor. I'm putting in a lot of money, and I'm going to want a lot in return. But I believe in you, and I believe in Mama Meg's."

Jack gave his head a little shake to try and clear out fantasy from reality, because he wasn't sure which was which. If he'd heard Allen right, Mama Meg's was being pulled back from the edge, again. When Jack thought the only option was to jump, Allen had shown him another way.

"You and Laura might need some time to talk about it," Allen suggested.

"Yes, we do. Can you give us a moment?" Jack replied.

"I'll step down the hall for some coffee and be back in about five minutes. Will that be enough time?"

"Perfect," Laura said. As soon as Allen had shut the door behind him, she turned to Jack, "We have to take it. Is there really any other choice?"

"I agree," Jack answered, "but I don't want to hand over nineteen percent share of our company so easily. That's huge."

"Jack, you can read the balance on that bank statement as well as I can. We owe a lot of money. I think this is a fair offer."

"What if we countered? Say, seventeen percent?"

"Or, we could offer fourteen percent with an option for five percent," Laura suggested. "That way he gets what he wants, but we don't have to give it away all at once."

"I like it," Jack replied. "You think he'll go for it?"

"If he doesn't, we can work something else out. Either way, we need this deal."

"I agree." Jack was still trying to catch his emotions up to the quick turn of events. Just moments earlier he'd been emotionally prepared to let Mama Meg's go. But now his mind was starting to race with all the opportunities Allen's investment would make.

There was a knock at the door and Allen let himself in. "All done talking?" he asked. "Did you figure things out?"

"We did," Laura replied as Allen took his seat again next to her.

"Nineteen percent is a large amount of stock," Jack said. "But I will admit we need your help. Would you accept fourteen percent stock and five percent in options?"

Allen narrowed his eyes at Jack, and Jack wondered if anyone had ever negotiated with him, or if he'd always gotten exactly what he wanted the first time he asked? "You really think you're in a position to haggle?" Allen's voice was brusque, hinting at irritation, but his mouth twitched up at the corner, telling a different story. The rest of his mouth finally gave in to the developing smile and he broke into a wide grin. "I accept. So, we have a deal then?" Allen stood and held out his hand. Jack took it, pumping with enthusiasm.

"Allen, I don't know what to say." Laura rose to move closer to the two of them. She reached out and took Allen's hand. "Thank you."

"I am not doing this to be nice, Laura. I don't take foolish risks. I've seen what you are both capable of and I see where you're taking the company. I want a part of that."

Just then there was a knock at the door and Chris poked his head in. "Oh, sorry," he said, looking just a little flustered at seeing Allen. "I didn't realize you were having a meeting. I just wanted to let you know that Gordon and his team worked their magic with my SCADA system and we've added several months to our timeline before we hit capacity."

"That's great to hear." Jack was beaming. "And Chris," he said, stopping him before he turned to leave, "let Gordon know we're going to need him to start working on extending the SCADA and work stations into the new plant. We'll be moving forward with the purchase as soon as possible."

Chris looked first at Jack, then Laura, in astonishment. Then he looked to Allen, who was leaning back in his chair with his legs extended, his arms clasped behind his head and a smug look on his face. "Got it," Chris answered. "I'll let him know right away."

13

The Edge

Two Years Later

The house lights were dimmed in the large ballroom so Jack, standing in the spotlight, could barely see anyone seated behind the second row. He straightened his notes on the lectern while the applause died down. He had attended the annual conference of the American Society of Baking for many years, but this was the first year he'd been asked to speak. He supposed winning Businessman of the Year had a little to do with why he was giving the keynote address.

"Two years ago, I never would have thought I'd be standing here before you as the recipient of this distinguished award. Instead, I was looking at the very real possibility of losing the company my mother had started and built from the ground up. But we survived and, today, we are stronger than ever.

"You may wonder how I was able to weather those storms and arrive at the place I stand, before you, today. Was it hardworking employees, dedicated executives and a solid business model that saved us? Absolutely. There is no way we could have overcome our challenges without those very important things. But, on their own, they wouldn't have been able to save us. No. The thing that kept us from being another mid-sized company to get gobbled up by a bigger corporation, the thing that made it possible for us to bridge that gap from regional bakery to sky's-the-limit, was our access to timely, accurate information. That was our edge."

Jack had come to understand over the last twelve months that even though money was the thing that pulled Mama Meg's back from the brink, Allen never would have made the investment if the company had been flailing. And without a strong technology foundation, they had definitely been flailing.

He contrasted the Mama Meg's before their IT overhaul— with spreadsheets, missed information and painfully slow communication—to the Mama Meg's *after,* with customized dashboards that had constantly updating data, linked modules that worked together to provide Sales and Manufacturing the numbers they needed to close sales and stay on top of production, and the accuracy and immediacy of communication throughout the whole plant. There was no comparison.

"With this change in the way we tracked and accessed information, our excellent employees, dedicated executives and solid business model became like a finely sharpened sword: Every cut cleaner, faster and more precise," Jack said, "we were able to develop new product and expand our territory. To put it bluntly, without that change, you wouldn't be seeing our cookies in twenty thousand kids' hamburger meals every single day throughout the United States. Hard work and the right information at the right time made that happen."

Jack was about to continue when a couple people started clapping and hollering. He smiled, recognizing Laura's voice among them. Quickly, the clapping caught on and spread throughout the room. He took it in, enjoying the moment.

"So? What's next for Mama Meg's?" Jack spoke once the noise subsided. "New products are in development; we are testing out several markets in Canada with great preliminary results. But best of all, with all this added business, we need to expand. So as of last week, the contract was signed to acquire our biggest competitor, Oven Love Baking Company."

Only a few Mama Meg's employees in the crowd, like Laura, understood the significance of this move or what had led to it. Ironically, it had been Burger Shack that had been Oven Love's undoing.

Burger Shack had required them to grow too fast before they had the infrastructure to support it. Their ERP system was outdated and underutilized; reports were still done on spreadsheets that were practically out of date by the time they were updated and distributed; and the different departments were disjointed and riddled with missed communications. None of this was too critical when they were small, but those methods could not sustain the business as they scaled up.

It sounded too familiar. The only difference was Jack had pulled things together with the help of Emmett, Tom and the Governance Committee. They'd been ready to take the Burger Shack account, and now they were ready to take Oven Love, too.

Jack recalled Leslie's especially taking pleasure in calling Soren to ask if he needed help with his job search.

Jack finished his speech to more applause and as he looked out across the room, his eyes now adjusted a bit to the dark, he found Laura in the crowd and smiled. Her grin was one of pure joy and for the first time, instead of wishing his mother had lived long enough to see this day, he felt grateful for all that she'd passed on to him: her knowledge, her work ethic, and especially her determination.

* * *

The hotel bar looked like it came out of a Swedish design catalog: made up of clean lines, aloof waiters and audacious light fixtures that would probably be out of style by next month. Laura was waiting for Jack in a quiet booth. He'd spent the whole day with a forced grin on his face, meeting and greeting. He was looking forward to some down time with a cold beer.

"Great job. You had them eating out of your hand."

"You think so? I could barely see anyone's faces to gauge how I was coming across."

"They loved you. Trust me." Laura took a sip of her cocktail. It was hot pink and looked like it would glow in black light. Something that might have been a flower petal floated on top. They sat in much welcome, comfortable silence for a few moments and then Laura said, "I almost forgot. Check this out." She reached into her bag and pulled out a magazine and pushed it across the table to Jack.

"What's Scott doing on the cover of *Outdoor*?" Jack knew Scott's river rafting business had been doing well, and ever since he'd started to work to get old dams removed, he'd become a local media darling. But this was a nationally published magazine.

"Pretty impressive, don't you think?" Laura asked. "His work here is gaining attention in other states and, believe it or not, our little brother has turned from the screw-up expert to an environmental expert."

"Unbelievable." Jack had been pretty sure Scott was throwing his money away when he bought that little river rafting business. Just another excuse to avoid responsibility, he thought. But after a few months it was obvious this wasn't another one of Scott's follies. Jack had never seen him so happy. Or exhausted. It was easy to see he was loving it. "I think Scott has actually found his calling."

"Keep the magazine. If you don't fall asleep brushing your teeth tonight, maybe give it a read before bed." Laura slid out from the booth and grabbed her coat. "I don't know how you're not asleep now. I can barely keep my eyes open. I'm headed up to my room."

"Thanks." Jack pulled the magazine towards him, glancing one more time at Scott's picture. He was standing on a riverbank, the white caps of rapids breaking over rocks behind him while he casually leaned on an oar. The sun was just setting over the mountains behind him and the light that filtered through the trees lit Scott up from behind so that he glowed. "I think I'll stay here just a little longer," Jack replied.

"Suit yourself," Laura said, turning to leave. She'd taken two steps when she turned back and said, "Honestly, Jack, your speech was fantastic."

He smiled as she turned and slowly faded into the crowd of bar patrons left over from the conference until he finally lost sight of her. He didn't have more than a few seconds to think about how much she had to do with Mama Meg's success, too, or how well he thought they worked together when a man approached Jack's booth and said, "Excuse me? Mr. McCallister?"

"Yes?" Jack replied.

"I was wondering if you have a minute. I heard your talk this evening and I was inspired. I'm Frank Atwood." He extended his hand and Jack took it. "I run Sweetie Pies, a small company that makes frozen pies using local, in-season ingredients. We have a very loyal following and are growing slowly."

Jack smiled. "Nice to meet you."

"I was wondering if I could ask you a few questions."

"Why don't you sit down," Jack said.

"Thanks." Frank slid into the booth across from Jack. "I won't take much of your time. It's late and I don't want to keep you. It's just that when I heard your speech, I couldn't help thinking about all the similarities between what you went through with your company, and what I'm seeing at mine."

Jack leaned forward in his seat. "Oh?"

"We are just starting up on a growth curve. I can see some of the problems you talked about already starting up. I need to avoid those, if I can. You seem to have done a great job staying strong while you scaled up."

Jack laughed at this, thinking back on all the near misses, the false starts, and the hard work. "We had our problems." He got serious then, thinking about Walt, whom he hadn't heard from in at least a year. "We definitely had our problems."

Frank nodded, more solemn now. "I would love to head off some of the problems before they become problems, if you know what I mean."

"Let's talk about your business plan, your business model and your infrastructure. These were all things we had to fix before we could sustain growth." Jack reached into his coat pocket, pulled out a card and handed it to Frank. "Call me and we can arrange a time to talk about it more. I'd be happy to tell you everything I know."

Concepts Tutorial

This section provides short tutorials on these topics:

- IT Governance
- Access Information/Dashboards – Business Intelligence
- Outsourcing strategies
- ERP systems
- CRM systems
- IT Project Management
- The right IT leader for your organization
- Managing IT risks

The tutorials are intended to be short and easy to read. Reading this section will provide you with a wealth of information for how to maximize the benefits of technology in your company.

IT Governance
(Managing IT for Maximum Business Benefit)

Business executives intuitively understand the importance of Governance for organization assets such as human capital, financial assets and physical assets. But they don't necessarily appreciate the need to govern information and IT assets. Given the intangibility of information and the resources invested in IT by the average business, it makes perfect sense to govern IT assets to control and mitigate risks and ensure performance.

Sometimes things don't go well in IT. There are obvious failures such as an expensive failed IT project or a disaster in which important business data is lost. Where does the fault really lie? Business executives are often puzzled by the complexity, costs and challenges of a constantly changing technology landscape. Frustrated with IT, they find it easy to abdicate decision-making for key IT decisions to their IT people. However, doing this is a mistake, one that most certainly leads to an underperforming IT organization. And low ROI on technology investments.

IT governance can be defined as the set of mechanisms and processes any business organization must set up to make key decisions about IT. In their HBR paper published in November 2002, Weill and Ross argue that there are several key decisions that business leaders should never delegate to IT. These include: How much money should we spend on IT? Which business areas should receive our limited IT resources? and What security and disaster risks will we accept?

IT has tremendous potential to help your business. In your organization, IT is comparable to a very sophisticated tool box in your home. Unfortunately, many people buy tools that they do not fully use. Perhaps in a home environment that may be okay but in a business setting that is unneeded waste and can prove to be fatal in some instances when the tool is misused.

How to Get Started Governing IT in Your Organization?

IT has many facets and its business value can only be measured and interpreted by business executives. IT governance has to be done by committee – usually called the IT steering committee. Take the following simple steps:

1. Form an IT steering committee consisting of key stakeholders of IT.

2. Develop a simple charter for the IT steering committee including goals, expectations, membership, roles and responsibilities and mechanisms for risk assessment, increasing alignment, monitoring performance and resource management.

3. Have the committee meet monthly initially with an agenda to discuss key IT projects, assess progress and take corrective actions where necessary. A goal of the committee should be to become tech savvy and learn how IT can be leveraged further for business.

4. Define an IT scorecard for the business. Perform a full annual evaluation of IT's contribution to the business. Use outside resources if needed for this step.

Doing all of this may sound like a lot of work in any organization. Some executives may think this is the task of the CIO or IT leader in their organization. This cannot be further from the truth. Since IT has so many dimensions and affects almost everyone in an organization, IT governance cannot be done solely by the IT leader in any organization.

Assessing IT Governance Maturity in Your Organization

As with any major change management effort, it can take years to implement changed business processes across organizations and get people to adopt new ways. Here is a simple way for organizations to know where they stand on the IT governance maturity scale:

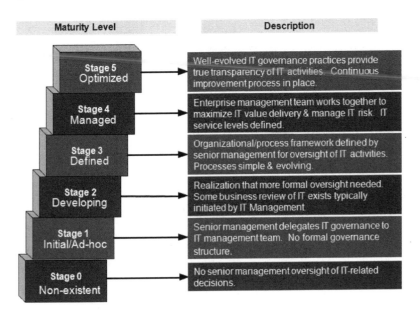

(Adapted from ISACA COBIT Framework)

Most mid-size businesses starting out will find themselves to be at Stage 0 or 1. The key to improvement is to know where you stand and work on making progress to the next level, which can take two to three years to implement.

When IT governance begins to work at any organization, many benefits are realized. First, business executives begin to make sense of the sometimes mysterious ways of IT. Second, they begin to work towards the good of the entire organization as opposed to optimizing only their part of the organization. Third, limited IT resources are allocated where they have the most impact on business. Finally, regular monitoring of key IT initiatives will uncover problems much earlier and they will receive the help needed from executives to get back on track.

For a more in-depth treatment of this topic, download our white paper, titled "How to Align IT With Your Business Needs," here: http://viellc.com/resources/

Questions for self-assessment:

1. Does IT in our organization seem to have too much to do without ever getting to any one thing effectively?

2. Have we had key failed IT projects? Do we understand why?

3. Is IT governance working effectively in our organization?

Access to Information
Dashboards and Business Intelligence

In most companies, there are multiple sources for data that can be used to generate reports that are used for decision-making. However, just having data doesn't necessarily mean that you have the appropriate information for making business decisions. You first need to define the Key Performance Indicators (KPI). These are the essence of tracking your business strategy and performance. Many companies have KPIs defined for various levels of management. For example, if yours is a manufacturing company, your production management people will probably need to know how many units are produced and how many are rejected due to quality defects. At the executive level you might be interested in knowing the progress the company is making on increasing market share and net revenue. Whatever the KPIs for your company are, you need to be able to measure them so you can get an objective look at where you stand in achieving your company's goals.

Once your KPIs are defined you'll need to look for a source of data for generating information about them. Your data sources will most likely be multiple operational databases. These databases are optimized for managing transactions and may not be suited for analytical reporting. In that case you will want to have a data warehouse built that is designed and optimized for data analysis and reporting.

Pieces of the Data Warehouse Puzzle

In order to build a warehouse system, a number of components need to be put in place to provide for the care and feeding of the warehouse.

Data Acquisition

The data acquisition part of the puzzle answers the questions: What kind of data do you have available to populate the warehouse? Where does it come from and how difficult is it to get? Data can be extracted from operational databases that you already have in-house. Data can also be acquired from external commercial information databases. Depending on what you want the database to do, you can use one or both of these sources.

Data Definition

Once you have determined where the data is coming from, you have to describe what it looks like and how it will be stored and summarized. This "metadata" is a crucial part of the warehouse and will determine what can be done with the data after it is acquired.

Data Scrubbing

Data from various sources can contain inconsistencies that must be removed before the data can be used for meaningful information. After the data is scrubbed it is integrated into a consistent structure and then summarized to speed the retrieval and analysis of the data.

Data Maintenance

After you've determined the source of your data you'll want to put in place a system to keep that data current. That will entail acquiring, scrubbing and summarizing the data on a regular basis.

Data Presentation

Once you have the data and it's been scrubbed and summarized, you need to do something with it. One of the best ways to use the data that you have gathered is a dashboard. A dashboard summarizes the data in a meaningful way and displays it so you have immediate access to the information you need to monitor progress on your KPIs. The data may be displayed in any form (graphs, reports, tables, etc.) that makes it easy to discern information about what you're most interested in.

Questions for self-assessment:

1. Have you clearly defined your Key Performance Indicators (KPIs) and are they measurable?

2. Are reports being generated mostly from the live IT systems or from a separate system (Data Warehouse) created for information reporting?

3. Do you have a Data Warehouse system that allows your people to pull customized reports as and when needed?

Outsourcing Strategies

There are lots of people looking at outsourcing these days as a potential cost-cutting measure. More often than not, outsourcing won't save any significant amount of money. What you will get is more value for the dollars spent.

The decision to outsource some or all of your IT infrastructure support is one that shouldn't be taken lightly or without a significant amount of due diligence when considering which partner(s) to work with. Managing and maintaining the portions of your IT functions that are critical, but not strategic, requires considerable time and effort. You have to think about what elements of IT are contributing directly to your company's business strategies and which ones are providing 'back-office' support. Both are important but optimally require different approaches. Those that are back-office support functions are probably the ones that are good candidates for outsourcing. The strategic contributors are ones you want to give more direct attention and resources. Even the strategic projects may have an element of outsourcing if you look closely at what items are one-shot tasks and which are ongoing.

The development of applications can be outsourced as well, but if you're developing applications, they are most likely competitive differentiators and you'll want to keep them close. If you happen to be developing an application that doesn't provide competitive advantage, you'd best look and see if it's worth doing at all.

When you start looking at IT infrastructure outsourcing, you need to know that there is a continuum of services that range from very little outsourcing to lots of outsourcing. There are three broad categories of outsourcing:

- In-house Managed
- Co-location Managed
- Fully Managed

Each of these categories has both positive and negative aspects and each should be considered when deciding on what outsourcing model works best for your organization.

In-House Managed

This category of outsourcing is probably the least costly because what you're paying for is remote expertise. You get the experts sitting at a partner site providing capability that you don't have on staff. In this environment, the partner you've selected will have connections to the systems that are on your site. They can monitor and manage the systems as if the partner personnel were located in your office. The great thing about this model is that you don't have to hire the specialist whom you may need only occasionally. The cost of that expert is spread across multiple clients and you're only paying for a tiny portion of the cost. The downside is that you may not get quite the same level of response to requests for service that you might with a dedicated resource. That can be mitigated by negotiating a service level agreement that provides for the response time that you believe you need and can afford. You also don't get the security of having your servers sitting in a hardened data center in the event of a disaster.

Co-Location Managed

This model is very similar to the in-house managed environment except the servers that run your business are housed outside of your offices. The advantage is that you will be more likely to have a robust physical facility with multiple sources of communication and power that will ensure that your systems are available in the event of a disaster. The downside is that you won't have quick, physical access to the machines. You're also paying for the physical plant, so it will be more costly than having the machines on-site. However, the odds are that you won't have the same level of physical security and reliability on-site, so you have to weigh that risk against the cost of a better environment. You'll still have the cost of owning and maintaining the equipment. You'll also have to pay, as in the in-house model, for expertise to manage your systems.

Fully Managed

In this environment, you don't own the servers and don't have to worry about whether they are up-to-date. You are paying for someone else to take on the technology refresh costs. You are also paying for the expertise to manage and monitor the systems. The systems you're using are housed in a risk-managed environment with backup power and communications. Again, this is more expensive than the other models, but you have to weigh that cost against the resources that you would be dedicating to the acquisition, management and maintenance of your systems.

Deciding On What to Outsource

In order to decide the right path for your organization, you have to understand the strategic business goals and how IT contributes to those plans. You also have to determine the risk that your company is willing to absorb and if outsourcing will mitigate or aggravate that risk. Reviewing the offerings of multiple service providers can be daunting unless you have a good benchmark to measure those services against. You'll need to negotiate a service level agreement that protects against poor service. All of these tasks take time and effort to do right, but if well done, can lead to a far stronger IT contribution to the company's business.

Questions for self-assessment:

1. Do you find yourself questioning the value of all the money you spend on technology?

2. Does your IT department seem to be spending an inordinate amount of time and resources just 'keeping the lights on'?

3. Do you believe that IT is a strategic business enabler or is it a cost center?

ERP Systems

Enterprise Resource Planning software, or ERP, is the holy grail of business software systems. It integrates all departments and functions in a company onto a single computer system, which provides each of those different departments with the information particular to its needs.

Until the advent of ERP systems, each department had its own computer system optimized for the particular business processes that the department performed. However, an ERP system combines them all together into a single, integrated software system that utilizes a single database so data can be more easily shared between departments. Doing this has huge positive implications for the company.

Take a supply chain order, for example, in a company without an ERP system. Typically, when Production runs low on a raw material, it places an order. That order may take a journey from the Production outbox to the Finance in-basket for approval and then to Purchasing for sourcing and so on around the company. Under the disintegrated pre-ERP model, the data would be entered into different computer systems along the way. While the order was sitting around in in-baskets with the concomitant delay, orders get lost, and all the entering into different computer systems along the way causes errors. Meanwhile, no one in the company truly knows what the status of the order is at any given point. For example, there is no way for the Production department to get into the Purchasing computer system to see whether the raw material has been ordered or shipped. "You'll have to call Purchasing" is the familiar catchphrase heard by frustrated production managers.

ERP systems replace all those old standalone computer systems in Purchasing, Finance, and Manufacturing, and supplants them with an integrated software system divided into software modules. Finance, Manufacturing and Purchasing still get their own software, but now the software is linked together so that someone in Sales can look into the Work-in-Process inventory to see when an order can be shipped. ERP software is flexible. You can install some modules without buying the whole package. In fact, the best way to implement an ERP system is to do it one module at a time. For example, you might just install a manufacturing or finance module. Once those are up and running, you can add a supply chain module or a sales management module; whatever makes the most sense from a business process improvement point of view.

Improving a Company's Business Performance with ERP

ERP's value can be demonstrated by looking at improvements in the order fulfillment process. When a sales person enters a customer order into an ERP system, she/he has access to all the information necessary to complete the order (the customer's order history from the sales module, credit rating from the finance module, the company's inventory levels from the inventory module and the trucking schedule from the logistics module, for example).

People in each of these different departments can all see the same information and know that a new order has been entered. The ERP workflow system moves the data along so that when one department finishes with the order it is automatically routed to the next department in the workflow chain. To find out the status of the order at any point, you need only look into the ERP system and track it down. With luck, the order process moves like greased lightning through the organization. Customers get their orders faster and with fewer errors than before. An ERP system can apply that same logic to the other major business processes, such as supply chain or production flow management.

Installing an ERP system is not an easy task and the changes that it engenders will affect your entire company; however, if done right, it will provide you with a wealth of data that can be used to put your company on an upward growth path.

Questions for self-assessment:

1. Do you find yourself frustrated by the lack of immediate information about what's going on in your company?

2. Are your business processes holding back company growth?

3. Does each department seem to operate in a vacuum without regard to the overall company goals and strategies?

CRM Systems

Customer Relationship Management (CRM) systems are used to learn and store information about customers' needs and behaviors in order to develop stronger relationships with them. Good customer relationships are at the heart of business success. There are many technological components to CRM, but thinking about CRM in primarily technological terms is a mistake. The more useful way to apply CRM is as a strategic process that will help you better understand your customers' needs and how you can meet those needs and enhance your bottom line at the same time. This strategy depends on bringing together lots of pieces of information about customers and market trends so you can sell and market your products and services more effectively. Although CRM systems are generally thought of as sales management tools and while they do perform quite well in that arena, they also serve as a Customer Service Management tool. Combining these two areas of customer interaction provides companies with a one-two punch when creating an environment that fosters customer satisfaction and loyalty.

CRM as Sales Management

When using a CRM system as a sales management tool, the Sales staff of the company has access to all the information about the interaction between the sales team and the customer. If the prospective customer has attended a webinar or visited a company exhibit at a sales expo, that information is captured and the company now has the information it needs to follow up on that lead. When the Sales staff calls or meets with the prospective customer, that information and any relevant information regarding the customer needs is recorded and available to Marketing and Sales Management for additional follow-up or marketing literature distribution. If the potential customer has a need that can be filled by the company's products and/or services, the inside sales people can develop a proposal to be delivered to the customer for their review and approval. If the customer declines the offer, the CRM system can capture the reasons for the lost sale for later review by both Marketing and Sales Management to discover weaknesses in both the sales approach and the product.

CRM as Service Management

Once a sale has been made, the specific information regarding the product sold can be entered into the CRM system and used for a wide variety of purposes. If there are upgrades to the product, the customer can be notified and additional revenue can be gained from the sale of the upgrade. If there is a defect, the product can be recalled easily and efficiently. When a product needs to be serviced, the service technician will be able to bring the right parts and tools to provide service to the customer.

Questions for self-assessment:

1. Do you know exactly how many prospective customers are at each stage of the sales process?

2. Do you know which customers have signed service agreements and when those agreements expire?

3. Can you quickly reach out to your customers with customized marketing messages about other products that they might be interested in purchasing?

IT Project Management

It is important to set up a structure that ensures project progress is reported to executive management on a timely basis. That structure consists of three layers: the executive management oversight team, the project steering team and the project implementation team. Each of these groups has a specific function in the success of a project.

The Executive Management Oversight Team, sometimes called the IT Steering Committee, is responsible for coordinating and prioritizing all IT-related projects company-wide. This group is typically comprised of the executive management team, including the CIO. They will typically invite Project Steering Team leaders to provide current status of projects underway. This team will meet on a regular schedule, typically bimonthly or quarterly, depending on the number and duration of projects that have been authorized. The meetings of this group can be contentious since each member of the management team has their agenda that they would like to see advanced. This is also a good forum for sorting out the relative strategic value of the projects under consideration. It almost becomes a review of the strategy and company goals.

The Project Steering Team sets project direction, allocates resources, monitors progress and oversees the project budget. This group consists of the leaders of all the stakeholder departments affected by the project as well as the executive sponsor and the project manager. This team will meet regularly on a monthly basis. They may meet more often if there are contentious issues that are unable to be resolved by the Project Implementation Team. There will be a project steering team for every major project in the company. If there are resource or progress issues that surface at this level, this team will resolve them if they can. If the issues are related to other projects or affect the business strategy, they may be referred to the Executive Management Oversight Team. This team has the primary responsibility for delivering a successful project on time and within budget.

The Project Implementation Team is where the rubber meets the road. This team is responsible for developing and managing the project plan that will meet the objectives of the project. The team consists of the project manager, direct stakeholders, and subject matter experts as needed. The project manager is the interface back to the Project Steering Team. This team typically meets weekly to discuss cross-departmental business requirements, prioritize implementation tasks, test system functionality and train other users. These individuals are responsible for communications with their departments. These are the people who have the most to gain from a successful project. Their departments will run better, their jobs will be easier and they will be more productive.

To recap, a good project management structure consists of three tiers:

IT Steering Committee

Role: Strategy, Project Prioritization and Funding

Members: Executive Staff and CIO

Project Steering Team

Role: Direction Setting
Resource Allocation
Progress Monitoring
Budget Management
Issue Resolution

Members: Project sponsor (preferably an executive staff member)
Project manager
Key management stakeholders
CIO (major projects)

Project Implementation Team

Role   Definition of functional requirements
Recommendations on direction and vendors
Implementation planning
Issue Resolution
Testing
Acceptance
Execution
Post Project review

Members   Project Manager
Subject matter experts
Technology experts
Key stakeholders

NOTE: Depending on the project size and scope, the Project Steering Team and the Project Implementation Team can be combined to eliminate duplication and make more efficient use of resources.

Questions for self-assessment:

1. How do you prioritize your projects and what criteria do you use to do that?
2. Are some projects arbitrarily prioritized ahead of the others?
3. Do you know what those projects are going to do for your business?
4. Do you have sufficient resources to successfully complete the authorized projects?

The Right IT Leader for Your Organization

Many mid-size companies struggle with realizing true value from their IT investments, including their IT Director. For a good description of the value to expect from IT, please see here (http://viellc.com/is-it-providing-value-in-your-business/). Part of the reason for this situation is that many executives think that the role of the IT Director is to "manage" the IT department. That is only part of the story. They should do a lot more.

Today, it is an inescapable conclusion that technology is a critical lever for business success. Most business executives know this but, because of the complexities of constantly changing technology, find it easy to delegate critical business decisions to their IT leader. This approach is fraught with danger, as now the key responsibility to ensure delivery of business value rests largely on the shoulders of the IT leader. Most IT leaders in mid-size organizations do not have the right skills to manage IT investments from a business perspective. They are usually more interested in technology for technology's sake and, at best, they work on providing decent IT services, not extracting the business value from IT.

Given this situation, with the large responsibility placed on their shoulders, it is critical to understand if your IT Director is capable of delivering the goods. So, what are some of the key attributes of a good IT Director? IT Directors typically manage a group of five to twenty-five people split into a few teams including infrastructure, applications and the service desk. They should have a strong technology background, but more importantly, they should be aware of the additional skills they need to develop to become a true business leader. Here are the five critical skills that an IT Director must have in order to be effective in their role:

- Communication and relationship-building
- Leadership and people development skills
- Strategic and planning orientation
- Project management skills
- Strong technical background and knowledge of IT processes and frameworks (ITIL, SDLC, PM, Security)

Unfortunately, some IT Directors who have strong technology skills lack necessary communication skills, especially with customers. Potential IT leaders must possess both complex technical knowledge and patience with those who do not have the same level of technical skills. Only IT people with this critical personality trait will be prepared to transition to a leadership role in the delivery of technology services. The best IT Directors are able to overcome their natural tendencies and develop a strong customer service attitude in serving their clients. Excellent IT Directors build excellent personal relationships with their customers in order to learn about business and challenges. This allows them to use their technical skills to design great solutions to add great value to the organization.

As technology people advance in their technical careers, there is a strong tendency to do things themselves to do it "right." When they assume a manager/director role, a strong shift in attitude is needed from doing things themselves to motivating and coaching team members to do a good job. This is a skill that may not come easily to someone who has been used to doing things themselves for many years. IT Directors need to be effective at leading people by setting the vision for IT and coaching and mentoring their people to give their best.

A critical aspect of the IT Director role is strategic and planning orientation. Although they may be involved in the day-to-day delivery of IT Services through the IT team, they need to maintain focus on the strategic impact and value of IT services. They can do this by learning as much as possible about the business, business objectives and metrics, strategic business initiatives and building an IT strategy that best supports the business. Having planning orientation is critical as it can be difficult to marshal IT resources in a hurry. Planning ahead for needs will go a long way to scaling the organization and meeting the needs of the business proactively in the most efficient way possible.

A 2012 McKinsey & Co. study of 5400 large-scale IT projects found that 17% of those projects go so badly that they threaten the company's very existence. On average, IT projects ran 45% over budget and over time, while delivering 56% less value than predicted. Project management skills are process-oriented skills that don't necessarily come naturally to tech people. For certain large projects, such as a major infrastructure upgrade or an ERP system implementation, IT Directors must have the right skills, such as requirements gathering, scoping solutions, estimating costs, figuring out return on investment, selecting resources to work on projects, scheduling and monitoring tasks. See here for a description of good project management practice (http://viellc. com/focus-on-why-to-drive-value-from-it-systems-initiatives/).

Finally, IT Directors must have broad knowledge of technical IT skills (networking, server management, IT security, cloud computing, IT application, etc.) in order to do their jobs effectively. As an IT Director, they don't need to know the details of any particular technology, just enough so they can direct the work of their team. In addition, since delivering IT services is now the work of a team, establishing a discipline of standard IT work processes using frameworks such as IT infrastructure library (ITIL), Software Development Life Cycle (SDLC), Project Management Book of Knowledge, and ISO 27002 for security, will be critical in organizing IT work and delivering cost effective IT services.

Questions for self-assessment:

1. Do we have trouble communicating with our IT leader? Does he or she speak a different language?

2. Has he or she managed our IT projects successfully?

3. Do we have a solid IT strategy written by our IT Director that aligns with business needs over the next two to three years?

Managing IT Risks

Organizations invest in long-term assets in order to utilize them to serve customers. These assets are valuable for the future of the organization and risks associated with these assets should be managed well. Information Technology is a key asset in any organization. Managing risks associated with IT is an important responsibility for business executives.

IT risks come in a few different forms. These include IT project risks, operational IT systems risks and information security risks.

The general steps to manage risks include understanding threats, assessment of the probability and possible damage for each threat, understanding methodology (process and technology) and costs to mitigate risks to acceptable levels and implementation of the methodology.

IT projects are notorious for not going well. Many formal studies have revealed that IT projects frequently fail to deliver promised business benefits. Some of them have gone badly enough to threaten the organization's viability. So, why are IT projects so difficult?

There are two reasons. One, IT systems projects always involve organizational change which can be very hard to implement. It takes a lot of persuasion to get people to change their behavior, even if they are convinced it is in the best interest of the organization. Second, by its nature, IT has a lot of moving parts and lack of formal project management experience causes organizations to make mistakes in estimating requirements, systems capabilities, timelines, costs and business benefits.

These sets of challenges, compounded, are the cause of IT project failures. In order to manage this risk, any business should employ formal project management techniques to manage IT projects. If these skills do not exist inside, then firms must hire outside professional project managers familiar with these types of projects. Further, firms must use the IT steering committee to review important projects frequently to make sure things are going well. If things are not going well, they may need to intervene with additional resources, changes in personnel or even cancel the project if it will not deliver business value.

Today, IT systems are critical for running any business. ERP systems provide the mechanism to store key information about customers, products and business process. They provide the workflow for the business to deliver products and services to customers and to generate revenue and cash flow. The possible failure of these critical systems represents a very large risk to any business. Most companies know that they should create business continuity and IT Disaster Recovery (DR) plans. However, we have found that, in the mid-market, almost ninety-five percent of firms do not have an adequate IT DR plan that would protect them in case of a disaster. Even though this represents such a large risk, firms seem to not want to "pay" for this kind of insurance. It is a big mistake. Creating a good IT Disaster Recovery plan is not complex. It just takes diligence to go through the process to create one. The process typically involves defining the scenarios for disaster. Examples of these include hardware and software failures; environmental failures, such as power and HVAC; and larger issues, such as natural disasters. Once the threats from these kinds of scenarios are assessed, a business impact analysis (BIA) will help to determine the needed time to recover systems and how much data loss can be tolerated. The BIA will also drive the appropriate level of investment in DR facilities. The next step is to implement the DR technology needed and to document the exact procedures for recovery for each of the systems considered. The DR plan should be tested at least twice a year to be relevant. The IT steering committee should ask for and inspect for the existence of an IT DR plan and the results of DR tests.

Information security risks have grown tremendously over the last decade or so. The need to share corporate data with partners, and the proliferation and complexity of information systems, have contributed to this state. Critical personal or corporate information could now be sitting on a mobile phone, a laptop or tablet, a web server, on the cloud or on an internal corporate server. Corporate and international espionage seems to produce new ways to break into systems almost every day. Breaches of critical data are now a headline almost every month.

So, how should organizations protect their critical information and reduce risks? By investing in a more formal process to assess risk, implement protection mechanisms and educate users about how to handle critical information. The International Organization for Standardization (ISO) 27000 framework provides a great set of guidelines for how to set up a security program in any organization. Regulations such as PCI, HIPAA, HITECH, GLBA and FERPA provide additional information and, in fact, require covered entities to follow certain rules and prove that their information is securely handled.

There are two steps to securing information. First, using the ISO standards, organizations must invest in the creation of a formal security program and process to manage security risks. Second, organizations must conduct an annual external third party audit to assess the adequacy of management and technical controls and implement corrective actions as needed. The IT steering committee should inspect for the existence of a security program and should review the results of the external audit and make sure that corrective action is being taken to control risks.

Questions for self-assessment:

1. Are we adequately managing IT risks?

2. Have we had any failed IT projects in the last few years?

3. Do we have a solid IT Disaster Recovery plan? Has it been tested twice annually?

4. Do we have a security program? Have we conducted an external audit? Have results been satisfactory?

The Edge - Author Bios

Manoj Garg is the Founder and Managing Partner of Virtual Information Executives, a consulting firm that specializes in helping clients achieve breakthrough business results through IT leadership. Manoj brings over thirty years of senior executive leadership skills and technology management experience with domestic and international operations to VIE's clients. Manoj's Information Technology (IT) experience covers a broad array of skills, including Large Scale Technology Infrastructure Management, Outsourcing Management, Information Security Management, Program Management and Enterprise Resource Planning.

Mike Scheuerman is a CIO Consultant for Virtual Information Executives. He brings over thirty-five years of senior executive leadership skills and technical expertise with domestic and international operations to VIE's clients. He has worked in multiple industries, including financial services, health care, high tech manufacturing and higher education. Mike's Information Technology experience covers a broad array of skills, including Outsourcing Management, Customer Relationship Management, Supply Chain Management, Business Intelligence and Infrastructure Management. He is noted for creating strategic business and technology plans that drive significant growth while also focusing on cost containment.